ARMCHAIR MYSTIC

Armchair Mystic

How Contemplative Prayer Will Bring You Closer to God

Mark E. Thibodeaux, SJ

franciscan
media®
Cincinnati, Ohio

Nihil Obstat:
Rev. Lawrence Landini, O.F.M.
Rev. John Armstrong, S.J.
Rev. David L. Zink
Imprimi Potest:
Rev. Fred Link, O.F.M.
Provincial
Rev. James P. Bradley, S.J.
Provincial
Imprimatur:
Most Rev. Carl K. Moeddel, V.G.
Archdiocese of Cincinnati
March 15, 2001

Cover and book design by Mark Sullivan

ISBN 978-1-63253-288-6

Published by Franciscan Media
28 W. Liberty St.
Cincinnati, OH 45202
www.FranciscanMedia.org

To Mom and Dad,
who first taught me how to pray

contents

They say you never get over your first love....

I began writing *Armchair Mystic* around 1999, which is to say that this work is now twenty years old. My first-born child is all grown up! Tens of thousands of people have read it, and it has been one of the blessings of my life to accompany them through the fits and starts, the ebbs and flows of their contemplative prayer lives. I have been delighted and enriched by the conversations that have flowed from it.

In a way, one could say that *Armchair Mystic* began even earlier. In the early 1990s, as a seminarian teaching theology to sophomores at Jesuit College Preparatory in Dallas, it struck me that while the school did a great job of teaching *about* God, it did little to teach our students how to *be with* God—how to pray and be in a relationship with God. So, with the blessing of my administrators, I added a new dimension to my theology class. From time to time, after calling roll, I would read out the names of half the class and say the words that every adolescent boy loves to hear, "Gentlemen, you are free to go." I would then take the other half into our small chapel to learn about and to practice contemplative prayer. The next day, I would do the same with the other half.

There were good days and bad days. I remember one particularly discouraging period wherein one of my would-be monks loudly passed gas and my other young monks could not regain composure for the rest of the period. I remember looking to the tabernacle and sarcastically saying to Jesus in my mind, "You know, if you cared to stop in and visit every now and then, I would really appreciate it."

Another struggle I had was finding good reading materials that were basic enough for teenagers to understand but not so simplistic as to bore them or insult their intelligence. I never found just the right book, so I resorted to writing handouts, using explanations, stories, and metaphors from my own experience of contemplative prayer. I had no notion these handouts would later become the foundation of a book.

After a few years of teaching, I moved on to the final phase of my pre-ordination formation: theology graduate school. I took a wonderful class called "Reading about Contemplative Prayer." I enjoyed it so much that I pitched an idea to my professors for an independent study that I called, "Writing about Contemplative Prayer." I would write a bit about one topic or another in contemplative prayer. I would then copy and distribute my writing to a diverse group of readers and would subsequently interview them about their experience after trying out what the written piece had instructed. I would then return to the work and reshape it based on what I had learned from my "experimenters in the field."

I smile when I recall some of the memories of bumbling through the writing of this first book:

The book was originally six long, ponderous chapters. My readers said, "It's good, but each chapter is a bit heavy—a bit too much to chew on in one sitting." That's when I had the epiphany of breaking it up into lots of smaller chapters. The problem was that it required "shattering" the chapters into small bits. How could I then put it back together again? I remember writing on scraps of paper torn out of my legal pad, the thesis statement of each potential chapter and laying them out on the floor of my bedroom. Until I got the arrangement just right, I sat there moving these pieces around in one order and then another as though I were arranging Scrabble tiles, searching for the elusive seven-letter word.

After spending weeks writing in my bedroom in Dallas, I began climbing the walls. So, using vacation money my superior had given me, I drove to Oklahoma City and checked into a Motel 6 for three or four days. I stopped looking at the clock and let the writing dictate when I would eat, sleep or write. My "days" became surreal, sometimes writing in the dead of night, sometimes sleeping deeply at midday. This crazed schedule worked brilliantly: I did some of my best writing in that cheap motel room.

Much later, months past my writing deadlines, I spent several days and nights alone in a snow-covered cabin in Massachusetts, putting the very last touches on the manuscript. On my last evening, I was sure that it was finally finished when—just before turning off my laptop and going to bed, I noticed a "hole" in one chapter whereby some yet undiscovered story should go. A while later, I knew just the right story: the one in which I sit on my dad's lap, homesick for our previous home, found at the beginning of Chapter Six. You would think I'd be happy about conjuring up this story, but I was furious! I knew that adding even a short and simple story would mean weeks of more of tweaking, editing and revising. And I was sick of writing and ready to be done with it all! I went to bed that night angry and convinced that I could leave the story out. But the manuscript, like a cranky child wanting to be fed, kept crying out to me. Now that the story was planted in my brain, I would get no peace until I wrote it. So, the next morning I rolled my sleeves back up and got to work again. Reading that story today makes me proud and happy that I did not finish the manuscript until the manuscript itself would tell me when it was finally ready.

I also have fond memories of the years that followed the book's release:

- *Armchair Mystic* will always be tied to my priesthood because it was published two months before my ordination. At my First Mass reception in my hometown of Church Point, Louisiana, in the midst of boiled crawfish and live Cajun music, I signed so many copies of my book that I had to sneak out of the back door of the Knights of Columbus Hall just to take a break.

- One of my Jesuit buddies sent me a meme of a skeleton covered in cobwebs and sitting in an armchair. "You forgot to tell your readers to stand up when they're done!" he wrote. He also suggested that the sequel should be a horror story: *Armchair Mystic 2: Up from the Chair*!

- Years later, after publishing my second book, I once met a quirky sacristan in Denver who told me that her women's group had read both of my books. "Most of them loved *Armchair Mystic*," she said, "but I'm more of a *God, I Have Issues* kind of girl." One of my novices at the time thought this was hilarious and frequently referred to himself as a *God, I Have Issues* Kind of Girl.

When the folks at Franciscan Media and I began discussing what changes we might make to this new edition of *Armchair Mystic*, we decided to leave the text almost completely as it is in the original edition. We felt that people liked the book for its personal, two-friends-talking-over-coffee kind of style. We felt that there were many Armchair Mystic kinds of girls and guys out there who like the book just as it is. The book is now as much theirs as it is mine, and we wouldn't want to alter it in any significant way.

So instead, we decided to leave the original text alone and

simply to add a couple of things to this edition: this preface telling you about my personal relationship with this wonderful "first-born child" of mine, and an afterword, giving you a few of the new ideas I've had in the twenty years since the writing of this book.

Enjoy!

O Lord, my heart is not lifted up,
my eyes are not raised too high;
I do not occupy myself with things
too great and too marvelous for me.
But I have calmed and quieted my soul,
like a weaned child with its mother;
my soul is like the weaned child that is with me.
—Psalm 131:1-2

Most Christians operate under the assumption that there are two difference types of prayer. First, there is the prayer of the everyday person. For example:

- Rushing to class, the college kid asks God for help with the upcoming literature exam.

- For reasons unknown even to herself, the middle-aged attorney spends her short lunch break at Mass in the little chapel three blocks from her office.

- As the sun rises and his baby girl wakes, Dad prays the Morning Offering and asks God to keep his daughter strong and healthy.

And then there is the prayer of the holy people—of monks and nuns who spend their lives very close to God, spiritually lifted to a heavenly place through some sort of otherworldly prayer that bears no resemblance to the prayer of the common man and woman.

This book calls this whole mindset into question. This book assumes that:

- Holiness comes in all shapes, sizes and walks of life. The father gazing on his sleeping child has as much potential to be holy as the monk gazing upon the tabernacle.

- There is no great divide between the prayer of the monastery and the prayer of the marketplace. There is no fundamental difference between the frantic pre-exam prayer of the college kid and the quiet prayer of the monk contemplative.

Contemplative prayer is not about leaving this world. It is not an otherworldly experience. Those who pray contemplative prayer accept and embrace *this world* and the Creator who dwells therein.

Contemplative prayer is not exclusively for monks and nuns. The college kid, the father, the lawyer and all everyday people *can pray contemplatively.*

This book does *not* assume, however, that contemplative prayer "is so easy that anyone can do it." Contemplative prayer is not necessarily easy. In fact, there are parts of the experience that are very difficult. But the point is that if I have the strong will and desire to pray contemplatively, I do not have to shave my head and join a monastery to do it. The armchair in my house is just as capable of being the holy ground of contemplative prayer as the monastery stall of a cloistered church.

If you are an everyday person who feels called to a deeper experience of prayer, then I encourage you to read on. Perhaps you are called to begin to pray contemplatively. This book can give you a few pointers to help you get started.

OVERVIEW OF THE BOOK

Practically speaking, how do I proceed?

The first chapter lays down a few of the preliminaries of prayer—the logistical details that need to be established before beginning to pray contemplatively.

Chapters Two through Four serve as an introduction to contemplative prayer. They present the basic characteristics of prayer and the general thrust of the movements of a person's prayer life. Chapter Two spells out how a typical contemplative prayer life usually evolves, from my first words to God to God's last ones to me. I present the maturation of the prayer life in four stages that are analogous to the stages of my own childhood maturation. Chapter Three speaks of the general direction in which I am going as my relationship with God grows deeper and richer. It presents my journey of prayer as a gradual surrendering of control of my entire life—including my prayer life—to God. It allows God to be God by letting him continue his creative action within me. Chapter Four speaks of solitude, the bread and butter of a contemplative relationship with God, and tells why it is necessary to learn to quiet the body and soul.

Chapters Five through Seven elaborate on the first three stages of my prayer life that were introduced in the Aunt Sally chapter. The fourth and final stage is very different from the other three, and typically a pray-er[1] does not fully experience this stage until later in his or her prayer life. Since most contemplative pray-ers spend the vast majority of their prayer lives in stage three, the discussion of stage four is reserved for near the end of the book.

Again, because most of the prayer life is spent here, Chapters Eight through Ten are really a further elaboration of stage three, Listening to God. These three chapters present the various ways of hearing God's voice, and they explain how I might better discern what it is that God is saying to me.

Chapters Eleven through Thirteen deal with apparent difficulties in prayer. Specifically, Chapter Eleven deals with temporary distractions in my prayer. It suggests a particular attitude to adopt in regard to distractions and then gives concrete tips on how I might deal with the distractions. Chapters Twelve and Thirteen deal with the more crucial situation of dryness in prayer—that is, the sometimes-long periods of my prayer life when nothing seems to be happening. It explores why God might allow such a difficult experience and what I can do to persevere in the midst of it.

In Chapter Fourteen, I return to the fourth stage of prayer, the stage of Being With God. Because this chapter speaks of the ultimate goal of prayer, it serves as a sort of overview of the entire adventure of contemplative prayer.

Chapter Fifteen concludes the book with an explanation of how my experience of God in prayer *must* be lived out through the love I show for my everyday world in the ordinary moments of my day.

Lest the reader lose track of the big picture, I begin several of the chapters with an Orientation, which places the particular topics at hand in the context of the whole book.

Step-by-step exercises are sprinkled throughout the book to provide concrete examples of how I might integrate into my prayer life the concepts presently discussed. They are lettered from A to V. An index of all of the exercises can be found after the Table of Contents.

How to Read This Book

As is clear from the above overview, the book proceeds in a systematic order. One chapter logically flows from the chapter that precedes it and prepares the reader for the chapter that follows it. For this reason, I should read each part slowly and pause to reflect on it awhile. I should not move on to the next part until I feel ready. On the other hand, some of the points made in the book will not make sense to me until after I have had some firsthand

experiences of contemplative prayer. So, if after spending time
with some particular part of the book, I still do not feel that I
have a good grasp of the point of it, I simply move on to the next
part. Later, as my prayer life grows, I can return to the book,
specifically turning to the parts that resonate well with whatever I
am presently experiencing in my prayer.

NOTE

1. Throughout the book, I use the term *pray-er* to mean "the person who
prays." As far as I know, this term was first used by spiritual writer, Father
Thomas H. Green, SJ.

chapter one

TIME, PLACE AND SPACE
The Nuts and Bolts of How to Begin

There are a few things that must be established before I begin any discipline or art—whether it be music, sports, cooking, or juggling. I must first understand what is required of me in time commitments (fifteen minutes or two hours?), what equipment I will need (a violin, a helmet, a blender, or three flaming torches) and what physical space I will need in order to practice and perform (a stage, a field, a kitchen, or a fire-resistant mat). Prayer is also a discipline and an art, so before getting into the *why*, the *what* and the *how* of contemplative prayer, it is necessary to discuss the *how often*, the *with what* and the *where*. This chapter discusses some of these nuts and bolts required before beginning the art and discipline of prayer. First, the values of commitment and of ritual are presented. Then, miscellaneous questions are explored.

CALLING AND COMMITMENT
Each Christian needs half an hour of prayer each day, except when we are busy...then we need an hour. —Saint Francis de Sales

Throughout my early prayer life, there were periods when the last thing I was in the mood to do was communicate with the "Almighty Creator of the Universe." It wasn't that I doubted God's existence or his love for me; it was simply that I was bored with prayer. Like the memory of tasting bad food, I recall lying in bed on numerous late nights, realizing that I had not prayed that day. I had no desire to get up and do so—even for a few minutes.

Instead of dealing with this problem forthrightly, I played a game I call Does It Count? A few of my fancy moves included: "I spoke with my spiritual director today. I suppose that counts." Or "I thought holy thoughts on the way to class this morning. Maybe that's enough." Or even "The priest's homily was double the length it should have been. That was more than enough!" It should come as no surprise that, although I grew better and better at my prayer-skirting plays (I had almost gotten to the point where God owed me time), I also grew more and more frustrated and unhappy with the whole prayer thing.

It all came to a head one hot summer night as I was sitting on a metal folding chair staring out at the nothingness of an El Paso desert. "What's wrong, God?" I asked him. "Why do I find myself playing these stupid games in order to avoid you?" As the prayer time went on, I gradually became aware of God's love enveloping me. It was not magic—there were no divine digits from the hand of God descending from the clouds. No, it was just a quiet, simple sense of his love. I felt a warm wind on my face and knew it was God's breath, breathing new life in me as he did with the dust that was Adam. Out of the dust devils of El Paso, I, too, was being re-created.

Well, that's a beautiful feeling, but I've had touching moments in prayer before. And unlike my earliest days of prayer, I was now painfully aware that there would be days when this wind would not blow, and I would be sitting by myself in the desert of dry prayer, sweating from the heat of loneliness. "What of those days, God? How do I stay loyal to you then?" I asked, seemingly interrupting God's breezy love song to me. But the wind still blew. And in it, I heard God's counter-question to me, "*Mark, what is it that you desire?*" It was the same question Jesus asked the two disciples when they followed him home one day (see John 1:35-39). It was the same question he asked the blind man, Bartimaeus (see Mark 10:46-52), and the lame man at the pool (see John 5:1-9). Now God was asking me.

God's question, "What do you desire?" was not the move of a manipulative mother using guilt to get her child to do some unpleasant task. No, God really wanted me to do exactly what I desired to do. He wanted no more than what I wanted. It was as though his sole purpose was to fulfill my deepest desires. "I release you," he seemed to be saying, "from whatever obligations you feel you have to accomplish for me. I promise to love you always—even if you never turn your face toward me again."

I was rocked even more by the response that was slowly forming inside me. "I want to be with you, God. I want to be at your side." I did not consciously choose to answer this way. It seemed to rise naturally from some place deep inside me, from below the surface of my superficial emotions.

From that day forward, a strange thing happened. I put away my game pieces and began to live a new prayer life. It was as though God had to free me before I could freely give back to God. I still had days when I didn't feel like praying. But even on those moody days, I could sense, just below the surface of my emotions, that deeper desire to be with God. And so with peace in my heart, I shushed my childish moods and prayed. The absence of the Does It Count? game brought me so much consolation that one day I promised God, "I will not let my head hit the pillow without spending exclusive time with you." This little vow has been my refuge from the silly games I played as a young pray-er.

GIVE IT YOUR BEST SHOT

When the subject of prayer comes up in conversation, someone will inevitably say, "Well, I don't get around to sitting still and praying very often, but I've come to realize that every moment of my day can be a prayer." This is absolutely true, of course. Having a sense of God's presence in every moment of one's day is even more basic to one's relationship with God than any particular type of prayer, such as contemplation. But the problem with that statement is that it implies that I have to choose one or the other: a prayer life (spending exclusive time with God every day) or a prayer*ful* life (acknowledging God's presence in every moment). A person who feels called to contemplative prayer rejects this either-or attitude and chooses *both* a prayer life *and* a prayerful life.

All Christians are called to pray, but in order to have a contemplative prayer life, *I must be called to it by God.* I must have a vocation to contemplative prayer in the same way that one has a vocation to marry a particular person, or to become a nun, a priest, an athlete or a parent. This is an important point to consider because it may well be that I, the reader of this book, am not called to contemplative prayer. Many people turn to a book like this more out of a sense of guilt than out of a sense of calling. They feel that they are bad Christians or that they are going to hell because they don't pray enough. If I am one of these people, then the Bible has very good news for me: Jesus has freed me from the law![1] God will love me regardless of whether or not I pray in *this* particular way. God does not desire me to feel obligated to spend time with him. Who would want such a relationship?

God does not call everyone to this particular type of prayer. There are lots and lots of good, happy and holy Christians who do not pray contemplatively. I may be one of them. For this reason,

I should ask myself if I really feel *called* to this—whether I feel a great desire to pray more deeply—or if I've come to it reluctantly and only because I feel that I *should* do it. I should try to answer this question as objectively as possible and drop any notions that I will be holier if I pray like the monks do. If God is not calling me to contemplative prayer, then it will not make me holier.

Perhaps I feel inclined to think that I am called to this, but I am not even sure what it means to pray contemplatively. Then I might give it a try for a while and see how it feels in my heart. But if I do choose to give it a try, then I must give it my best shot. *I must commit myself to pray every day.* I should skip over the silly games described in the El Paso story above. Those games will do nothing but frustrate me. Even if I want to just try it out, I will have to pray this way every day for quite a while before I can get enough of a taste of it to determine whether or not this type of prayer is for me.

If I am going to try contemplation at all, then I should jump into the pool with both feet and not just stick my big toe in. As with all disciplines, whether athletics, music, scholarship or whatever, I've got to give it my all in order to give myself a chance to know whether or not it's right for me. Otherwise, I would be like a high school kid who tells the coach, "Well, I'll give football a try. I'll practice a couple of days a week and play in a few games and then see what happens."

THE VALUE OF RITUAL

An elderly widow friend once told me that she thinks of her husband most when crossing a bridge. She explained that early in their long life together, she and her husband developed a habit of kissing each other every time they crossed a bridge. She could not remember how this little ritual began, but they were always faithful to it. "If he was driving and the traffic was heavy, we would have to wait for the next stop, but we never forgot about our kiss," she said. To this day, she cannot cross a bridge without sensing his presence.

Humans are creatures of ritual. For all the talk of spontaneity, people really like doing things the same way each time. It's a way of having continuity in their lives—of linking past events with the reality of the present and the hope of the future. With the repetitive gesture described above, this couple was saying to one another, "My love for you is the same yesterday, today and tomorrow." Also, ritual allows desirable inner movements to happen more easily and naturally. My friend did not have to resurrect her loving feelings toward her husband because ordinary events in her day (like crossing a bridge) naturally evoked them. Finally, ritual "sacramentalizes" the concrete world. It creates a "bridge" between the transcendent (this couple's sacred love) and the ordinary (a drive to the grocery store). For these reasons, it is a good idea for me, as a beginner in contemplative prayer, to set up some little rituals for my prayer life.

Here are a few suggestions:

- *I pray in the same place and position every day.* I experiment with different spots until I find the one that works best. Most people prefer a comfy straight-back chair (such as an armchair or a recliner) in a dimly lit room. I might add an object or two (for example: a candle, a cross, a picture, a prayer shawl, a memento) to mark the place as special.

- *I pray at the same time every day.* I experiment to figure out what time of day is most amenable to me (that is, when it is easiest for me to quiet myself). Many find the early morning best for solitude, but this is by no means a hard and fast rule.

Praying at the same time every day may also help those I live with to know when to "lay low."

• *I begin and end my prayer in the same way every day.* God told Moses at the burning bush, "Remove the sandals from your feet, for the place on which you are standing is holy ground" (Exodus 3:4ff.). Saint Ignatius of Loyola suggests that the pray-er "reverence his spot" before praying,[2] so, I bow, genuflect, or kneel before my own holy ground. I end the prayer time with the Sign of the Cross, the Our Father or some other prayer I like (or I make up my own).

I shouldn't think of these suggestions as rules. Doing so will turn lovely rituals into obligations. I should allow the rituals to change and to grow as my prayer life evolves. And I shouldn't be afraid to suspend some particular aspect of them because of extenuating circumstances (for example, a friend is sleeping on the couch where I usually pray). Life is messy. As long as I am faithful to my commitment, the details are just...well, details.

MISCELLANEOUS QUESTIONS

What if I am a college student who shares a dorm room, or a mother of three lively and loud children? Setting up the proper time, place and space for prayer may require a somewhat awkward conversation with the people with whom I live. This may be one of those moments when God asks me to stand by my priorities. On the other hand, if there is no way to guarantee quiet in my home, perhaps I should search elsewhere for a quiet, comfortable place. It should be easily accessible practically every day. Some potential spots include:

a bench in a nearby park

a church or chapel on my route to work or school

the roof, basement or attic of my building
my best friend's apartment while she is at work
the back storeroom at my job
a classroom which is empty at the same time every day
the subway train or my own car while commuting to and from
work or school

What if my room or apartment is small and my "prayer chair" is the only chair in my house? No problem. There is nothing wrong with using my chair for other activities as long as I find a way to mark the prayer time as a special one. I, myself, have only one chair in my room. It is my prayer chair, my study chair, my snoozing chair—everything. But only when I'm praying do I cover myself with my lap quilt and light my candle. These two simple objects turn that ordinary spot into a sacred one.

What if my apartment is near a noisy street or under a clattery neighbor? Jesuit Father Anthony DeMello used to make his students pray amidst disruptive noise to show them that over time it can be easily tuned out. I have found that I can mentally turn loud and constant noise into "white noise," which in my imagination forms a protective covering around me.

What if I really am extremely busy every day and find it difficult to find a time slot for prayer? One significant change I made after "the El Paso conversion" was that I began planning my day around my prayer time instead of the other way around. Now, before setting my alarm clock at night, I plan what time I will reserve for the next day's prayer. If the day looks busy, I adjust my wake-up time accordingly.

If I'm a businessperson, perhaps I could schedule an appointment with God each day. I mean literally write in "J.C." in my appointment book. When his slot arrives, I turn off the light in my office, close the door and get to my most important meeting of the day. If I am a student, I do not let myself return from class without stopping by the campus chapel for a visit. If I exercise daily, I can simply attach my prayer time to the beginning or the end of my workout. After my morning jog, I can sit on the lawn chair in my backyard for a while.

What if my "prayer spot" is actually my morning workout? Is that OK? It would be better if I could choose some time in my day when I can give a hundred percent of my attention to God, rather than dividing that time with crossing the street or adjusting the exercise machine. But if I have no other options, then by all means, I should use my exercise time. One advantage to praying while exercising is that its repetitiveness allows for a nice rhythm in my prayer. This is especially true about praying while on a stationary machine.

What if I fall asleep during prayer? If my falling asleep is only occasional, then I simply enjoy the rest. I consider it a gift from God. The psalmist did so when he prayed, "I have calmed and quieted my soul, like a weaned child with its mother" (Psalm 131:2). If I fall asleep very often, then perhaps I need to adjust (a) the time of day I choose to pray, (b) my prayer place and body position and/or (c) the amount of sleep I get at night. If all else fails, I pray on my feet, standing or walking.

For how long should I pray? That depends on my previous experience of prayer. If I've never prayed on a regular basis before, I may have to start out with five or ten minutes a day until I grow accustomed to it. After a while, I can recommit myself to fifteen or twenty minutes a day, and so on. Ultimately, it would be best to pray for at least thirty minutes a day.

However, I should *start slowly!* If I am overly enthusiastic about prayer right now, I may feel tempted to set an unrealistic goal. Later, when the enthusiasm wanes, I will not have the ability to maintain this lofty commitment and will feel guilty and frustrated about it. It would be better for me to make a more modest commitment that challenges me, but not unrealistically so.

On the other hand, assuming this time commitment is reasonable, I should work hard to stick to it. I should beware of the Does It Count? game!

One Last Thing Before Beginning . . .

There is one more important point that must be made before proceeding further. I must always remember that I can no more approach God than an infant can approach its mother. When that baby sees its mother several feet away, he tries to reach her by stretching out his tiny arms toward her. But it is Mom who goes the distance and makes the connection. In the same way, my human capacity to reach across the great divide between the finite and the infinite is eternally inadequate. But from God's perspective, the gap doesn't exist at all. Like a loving mother, our Mother-God is ever present.

Because of his mother's faithfulness, the child of the loving mother soon becomes convinced that his reach is sufficient, and in a way he's right, isn't he? In the same way, all I need to do in order to reach God is to reach *for* God. I should do myself a favor and memorize this line: *To reach* for *God is to reach God*. I will have to remind myself of this whenever I feel tempted to believe that God will only come to me if I find the magic book, say the magic formula and become the perfect pray-er. I should trust that God is present to me any time I stretch out my feeble little spiritual arms.

Notes

1. Galatians 2:16,19-20 and the *Catechism of the Catholic Church* #1992. Hereinafter cited as CCC.

2. *The Spiritual Exercises of St. Ignatius*, Louis Puhl, S.J., editor (Chicago: Loyola College Press, 1951), 75, p. 35. Hereinafter cited as *SpirEx*.

chapter two

AUNT SALLY
The Four Stages of Prayer

The term *contemplative prayer* is a broad and historically complicated one. Various spiritual writers throughout history have used it to mean different things. What St. Ignatius meant by contemplation is not the same as what St. Teresa of Avila or St. John of the Cross meant by it. The next three chapters present my understanding of contemplative prayer and explain the assumptions with which I am working throughout the book.

The present chapter describes how a prayer life might evolve over time.[1] I use a fable of my maturing relationship with "Aunt Sally" (who is actually an apocryphal compilation of several grandmotherly figures in my life), as an analogy for what happens as I mature in my prayer life.

TALKING AT GOD

I was four years old when Aunt Sally first came to visit. She was the kind of woman a kid imagines has always been old. Her whole face seemed to have slipped down a little, a downward smear like my chalk picture on the wall of the barn after a light summer rain. Her face had downward streaks, too, like the droplets of air-conditioned condensation creeping down the kitchen window. But her eyes were strangely bright and ever curious—much like a child's. In that cavernous face, they looked like monkeys dancing in cages.

But I was just a kid then and could not stand still to save my soul, so Momma always let me go after a few minutes of politeness. "Say, 'Hello, Aunt Sally'," my mom commanded me. "Hello, Aunt Sally," I responded—not looking at her for fear of her face falling off. "Tell Aunt Sally how old you are." I said nothing—just kicked the leg of the table with my foot. "Say, 'I'm four years old.'" "I'm four years old," I said, "Can I go play, now, Momma?" Ignoring the question, she asked, "Why don't you teach Aunt Sally a song?" Silence.... "Teach her 'I'm a Little Teapot.'" I hated that song. Marty's brother had laughed at me the last time I had sung it. "Sing 'I'm a Little Teapot' and then you can go outside and play," Momma said. I took a long pained sigh of resignation and began, "I'm a little teapot, short and stout...."

The first stage in the evolution of prayer is *Talking at God.*

Many of us learn to pray in the same way: You kneel by your bedside, fold your hands reverently, tilt your head in the same way Jesus does on that statue in church and you say, "Now I lay me down to sleep...." Being the youngest child in my house, I often led the grace before meals. With great theatrics, I would touch my forehead and begin, "In the name of the Father, and of the Son, and of the Holy Spirit. God is great. God is good. Lettuce thank him for our food." It wasn't until much later that I asked Momma why we thanked God only for the lettuce.

As a small child, I did not have the capacity to sustain conversations with God. Instead, I learned to simply parrot what my elders said. Before long, I had a few important prayers down: the Our Father, the Hail Mary, the Glory Be. These simple formulas serve for a lifetime of prayer and are as important as remembering to say "Hello, Aunt Sally." They are the foundation of my conversation with God. The actual words are not as important as the expression of my intent to be in relationship with God.

Consider the following dialogue of two acquaintances passing each other on the street:

"Hey Roberto, how are you?"

"Fine, Jim, and you?"

"I'm OK, but it's a little too hot for me."

"You said it. Do you think it'll ever let up?"

"This is Louisiana, remember?"

Jim is not necessarily all that concerned with Roberto's well-being and neither of them is really that interested in meteorology. And yet, these familiar phrases are important because they do convey a message. They say, "I can't talk now, but I do wish you well and hope you have a nice day." These phrases also come in handy when I am a little nervous or uncomfortable and do not know exactly what to say. In the same way, ready-made prayers like the Our Father and the Hail Mary are a way of letting God know that, "I can't talk now (because I'm tired, angry, confused, scared or maybe I just don't know how), but I do care about our relationship and I want it to grow."

But if God is all-knowing, shouldn't he already know this, and if so, why do I have to say anything at all? It's true that God knows this, but I must continue saying it for the same reason a husband must continue telling his beloved wife of many years that he loves her. It's not so much to give her factual information as to express his love in some concrete fashion. By saying, "I love you," to his wife, he is actually participating in an act of love. In the same way, saying ready-made prayers is not so much about giving God information as about performing an act of love for God. That is why I say that the words of the prayer are not as important as the sentiment they convey. When I, as a child, prayed, "lettuce thank him..." and even thought about lettuce, I am quite confident that, though the words were incorrect, the prayer was fine. God *is* all-knowing, so he can read the intentions beneath the prayer.

When do I find such prayers useful? When I am traveling, for instance, I often find precious little time to spend alone with God. Often by the time I get to pray, I am exhausted from the concerns of traveling and I do not have the strength to have a conversation with God. And yet, I do not want to go to bed without consciously reaching out to him. Like a burnt-out couple at the end of a long day of caring for children, I simply say, "I love you" with my Our Father's and my Glory Be's and then go to bed. Another time I find these prayers useful is when I am in the middle of a crisis and am emotionally fragile. If my brother has been in a terrible accident and is in the hospital, I may be too broken up to find the words to pray. That is when I use these recited prayers, allowing them to provide the words of my prayer.

There are also less traumatic moments of my life when I find it difficult to do anything but traditional prayer. I remember one such occasion a few years ago when I knew that I would have to confront a friend about some serious problems between us. I had prayed about this for several days and felt it was the most Christian thing to do. However, the day that I was to talk to him, I grew very nervous and ill at ease. I wanted to sit quietly and speak to God from my heart, but every time I sat still, I grew more and more nervous. So I grabbed my rosary and went for a walk instead. It was a great consolation to have Mary pray for and with me at this time.

There is yet another reason to pray this type of prayer. When I do so, I am using the ritual nature of it to unite myself with millions of other Christians who will pray the same prayer that day, not to mention the billions who have prayed these prayers throughout the history of Christianity. God calls me to be in community. "No man is an island," as John Donne has written. To know that I am approaching my God with my Christian sisters and brothers around the world and throughout history is a wonderful consolation to me, especially in the more difficult times of my life.

TALKING TO GOD

The next time Aunt Sally came to visit, I was a few years older and had come to discover that I was the center of the universe and that all of creation revolved around me. I lived under the assumption that everyone was as fascinated with every detail of my life as I was. That is why I did not protest when Aunt Sally placed me on her lap and asked me to tell her all about the picture I had been drawing on the floor when she arrived. This question of hers was the spark plug that set my motor mouth running. I showed her the picture of me with hatchet in hand and explained that I was a great lumberjack and would chop down hundreds of trees in a day. I would chop down only the bad trees of course—the ones that were dark and scary and would not allow any birds or squirrels to live in them. I showed her the deep, dark woods in my picture and explained to her that I was just about to enter that forest and free it from those terrible trees. She asked about the eyes that were peering out of the darkness of the trees, and I explained that they were the eyes of a great big monster that served the dark trees and would have to be chased away. She asked if the monster scared me, and I told her that sometimes at night I would see his eyes looking at me outside of my window and it would scare me very much. A couple of times I even had to run to Momma and Daddy's room for the night. But in the daytime I wasn't scared, and I was gonna chase that mean old creature out of there this very day.

Throughout the entire story, Aunt Sally listened with great attention and clicked her tongue and nodded her head at all the right times. When I spoke of the dark creature, she put on a serious face and nodded gravely as though she were a fellow soldier in battle, receiving hard news from the front. A few times she tried to interject her own experience of forests. She wanted to tell me about the lovely bluebonnets that she used to pick in the clearings of the woods and about the family of rabbits she discovered once. But I was too wrapped up in my own stories to hear about flowers. There were monsters to master and I was just the man for the job. So I never let her tell a single story from home, but interrupted her very early in the story to revel in my own musings. She never seemed angry or disappointed about that. Instead, she simply grew quiet and let me take over the conversation, except for a few, "Really?'s" or "Is that so?'s."

Aunt Sally made me feel as though I was the only person in the world who mattered to her and that nothing I said, or felt or did was unimportant.

The second stage in the evolution of prayer is *Talking to God*.

As I mature in my relationship with God, I become more comfortable with finding *my own words* to speak to God rather than using the ready-made prayers of my childhood. I simply speak to God from my heart, straightforwardly telling him all about whatever is going on with me right now. I still pray and am enriched by my ready-made prayers, but now I also want to go beyond formal words written by someone else. I want a more personal relationship with God.

At the same time, I may feel a hesitancy to move to this stage in my prayer. For one thing, it may feel weird talking to a person who does not have a body. And because God doesn't have a body, he generally doesn't speak back with a human voice. So praying this way can feel as though I'm just talking to myself.

But if I overcome the initial feelings of discomfort, I will find spontaneous prayer a wonderful experience. God no longer will be simply an acquaintance with whom I say only my formal "Hello's." Like Aunt Sally, God will become my captive audience, hanging on every word that I say—accepting my thoughts and feelings without scrutiny or critique—and thereby loving me unconditionally.

This move to the second stage of prayer may also be difficult because what I have to share may not always be positive. I may be angry, upset, frustrated and so on, and I'm not too sure how God will react to these feelings. Consider again the dialogue between Roberto and Jim. What if, when asked, "How are you?" Roberto responded, "Well, Jim, things aren't so great right now. Do you have a minute to talk?" This would be a risky move on Roberto's part. How would Jim react? Insensitively? Angrily? There are a thousand ways Jim could hurt Roberto at this point. Perhaps Roberto would end up wishing he had just said, "Fine. Thank you." This is why many Christians are content with praying ready-made prayers alone. If I speak with God from my heart, how will God react? If I must watch what I say and how I say it in front of priests, ministers and nuns, how much more must I censor myself in front of God?

But in order to grow closer to God, I must take a leap of faith and trust that when God tells me he will never reject me, he really means it (see Isaiah 49). God loves me unconditionally and wishes for nothing more than for me to come to him with open hands and open heart, hiding nothing—sharing my joys and sorrows, my peaks and valleys.

LISTENING TO GOD

By the time I was thirteen, Aunt Sally had grown too old to live on her own and had moved in with us. I didn't know how I'd feel about living with an old lady, but before long, we had become the best of friends. At first, she let me do all the talking, as I had during her last few visits. But by this time I was old enough to realize that this old lady had a few stories of her own. I remember one day telling her how anxious I was to be old enough to drive. I launched into a long description of how good I was at driving my own go-cart, even through the fields, which lay fallow behind our house. As I was saying this, she quietly mentioned how much my story reminded her of the days she and her brother would hunt on horseback in the piney woods of East Texas. Well, I continued telling my story, but this hook of hers had sunk deep, and before long I found myself begging her to tell me more about those great Texas hunts. I don't know how many hours I sat there enraptured by her tales, because for me, time had stood still. This day marked the beginning of a routine, which lasted for years. I would come home from school, grab a plate of Oreos and a glass of milk, and sit on the floor pretending to watch *Bewitched*, but really listening to Aunt Sally tell me all about her beguiling life.

Hers was not an easy life. The family was quite poor and those hunting trips were as much out of necessity as out of fun and adventure. Food was scarce for them and many days went by with no substantial food at all on the table, only coarse cornbread and thin milk from the scrawny backyard cow. The funny part about it all is that her brothers and she had no idea that there was any other way to live. Everybody she knew lived this way.

She told many other stories: the day her brother ran off with the neighbor and got himself married, the day her father left for

World War I and the day he returned with one less leg, the day her husband left for World War II and the day she found out he would never return. She told happy stories, too: the day she first rode in an automobile, the night she got to lay the Baby Jesus in the crib at Midnight Mass and what it felt like to have the whole world watching as she held God in her hands and rocked him to sleep. She told me all about the village corn-shucking days and the slightly bawdy dances that followed them. It was at one of these that she stole her first kiss from Bobby-Ryan Wilson, who was so shy she had to practically drag him behind that barn to do so.

Those stories had a hypnotic effect on me, intoxicating me on the anecdotes of years gone by. She asked me questions about my life, too. But now, I answered them as quickly as possible so that we could go back to times and places I would only come to know through the tales of Aunt Sally.

The third stage in the evolution of prayer is *Listening to God*.

A child who has advanced from parroting words like "Momma" and "Da-da" to forming her own sentences has taken a great step. But she is still a child. The mark of a mature person is the ability to *really listen*. This is true, also, of my relationship with God. The Lord will never tire of hearing my voice. Like Aunt Sally actively listening to my monster-fighting musings, God is always ready to be my captive audience. On the other hand, he has many important things to say to me. He wants to share in my struggles and console me in the difficult times. He wants to challenge me to repent and to live the gospel more authentically. He wants to guide me through the decisions I make and to encourage me to live by those choices. He wants to celebrate my inner victories and to teach me how to have more. Mostly, he just wants to say, "I love you."

Obviously, a conversation with God is not like a conversation with Aunt Sally in that, in prayer, God does not usually come in human form or with human voice. So the question becomes, "How do I hear God's voice if that voice is not a human one?"

Two things are immensely valuable for a person to learn to discern God's voice. The first is *instruction*. What God wants to communicate to me in prayer is richer than anything human language can express, so God must use more subtle means. If I'm going to learn how to pick up on these ways of God, I will probably need to receive instruction from those who are a little farther down the road of prayer. Through spiritual guides in my life and through books about prayer I can slowly learn God's language of love. That is why a large section of this book, Chapters Seven through Ten, is explicitly dedicated to this topic.

Learning the language of God also requires a good bit of *personal experience*. Spiritual writers and speakers sometimes say things like, "God's voice is whispering in the rustle of the leaves and is singing to us through the melody of the birds." But these sorts of statements often drive beginners away, saying, "What the heck are they talking about? Birdsong is beautiful, but I don't hear any message from God in it." They may go away, believing that these "prayer people" are crazy and are hearing things that aren't there. Or they may believe that God has nothing to say to them and that they should leave the praying to monks and nuns.

But God does have his stories to tell and some of them are meant just for me. God wants to cultivate a deep and personal relationship with every one of his daughters and sons. However, relationships take time and they require the commitment necessary to really get to know another person. If Jim asks his good friend Roberto, "How are you?" and Roberto responds, "Things have been tough lately, but I'll be all right." What is Roberto really saying here? Is this a cry for help or merely a sharing of minor setbacks? Does Roberto always complain about his life or is this negative statement unusual and, therefore, potentially serious? I can't tell because I don't know Roberto, but if Jim has been friends with Roberto for a while and has been through good times and bad with him, he knows how to interpret such a statement. Likewise, *I will never be able to hear God's voice in nature, in other people or in the words of the Gospel if I do not know God. And I will never really come to know God unless I am willing to put in the time, patience and practice necessary for this (or any!) relationship to thrive.*

I remember a friend telling me once about her decision to marry her boyfriend. She knew that, for various reasons, I would disagree with her decision and would not be afraid to tell her why, so she never let me get a word in. Instead, she chattered away about how beautiful the wedding was going to be and what her dress was going to look like and on and on. Before I knew it, she was kissing me on the cheek and telling me that she had no more time to talk and would call me later. This is another reason many Christians never stop to listen to God: They are afraid of what he might say. The sad part about this is that people forget that God really does want what is best for his children. If on a trip I were to become lost, would I refuse to listen to someone who knows the way simply because the road to which she is pointing will require more gas? God knows the way to true happiness, and he wants me to know about it, too. I should not refuse him simply because his way is more demanding.

Being with God

Time passed and Aunt Sally grew older and frailer. The end of her life came slowly, after a prolonged stay in the hospital. It was my senior year in high school, and while all my friends were chasing girls and dreams of college life, I was sitting by my Aunt Sally's bedside. There were days when she was full of energy and would regale me with more stories of her past. But there were other days when her ever-curious monkey eyes didn't dance so vibrantly. Sometimes I would fill such days with my own tales, trying to make her laugh as payback for all the times she split my sides with funny stories.

But as the days turned into months we spoke much less. Whole days would go by in almost complete silence. Looking back on my life with Aunt Sally, it is the memory of those silent days that I now hold dear. I can't say how or why, but somehow those were the days when we were closest to one another, as though we had come to realize that the words we spoke simply crowded the room like unwanted guests. The silence, on the other hand, pulled us closer together like a sacred cord that bound us in ways beyond our control or understanding. When I tried to explain this extraordinary experience to my friends, I could never really make them understand just how it felt to have this invisible, fragile-yet-eternal tie with another person. At the time, I assumed my inability to explain it was because I was so young and inexperienced with such things. But now, years later, I still falter and am frustrated by the indescribable nature of it. But that is the point, isn't it? That is why, in the end, words were more of a hindrance than a help. These holy moments are beyond explanation, and that's what makes them so special.

The fourth stage in the evolution of prayer is *Being with God.*

This last segment of the Aunt Sally parable describes a crucial moment in any intimate relationship. It is the moment when *being* in one another's presence is more important than any particular activity I might do with that person. *What* I do with my beloved is irrelevant, as long as I can do it *with my beloved*. I do not need to do anything particularly entertaining or fulfilling because her mere presence in my life brings me fulfillment. Her presence makes any activity fulfilling.

In the same way, there will come a time in my long-term prayer life when the activity of my prayer becomes much less relevant. Merely resting in God's presence will be sufficient. Consider the first moment Mario lays eyes on the beautiful girl across the classroom. On the way out of class, Mario bumps into her and politely says, "Excuse me." He then strikes up a conversation with her about the class, the weather and so on (the first stage). After more chance encounters, they begin dating. Because he is nervous and is desperately in need of impressing her, Mario fills the time of their first few dates with a great deal of activity. One day they go to the movies, the next time it's biking, then it's bowling, and so on. All the while they are together, Mario nervously chatters away about anything and everything (the second stage). A couple of months later, Mario goes to Samantha's house only to find her in a dirty T-shirt and jeans. She explains to him that she has been gardening all day and would rather not go out that night. Instead, the two of them have leftover pizza in the living room with Mom, Dad and Little Sis. At one point, Mom brings out Samantha's baby pictures and the whole family has a ball regaling Mario with their family history. They are so kind and unassuming that Mario finds himself very relaxed and thoroughly enjoys feeling as though he doesn't have to do all the talking (the third stage). By their six-month anniversary, Mario and Samantha are spending most of their time sitting around each other's houses or going for quiet walks around the block. If one were to see Mario after one of these simple evenings and ask him about what he and his girlfriend had done that evening, Mario might just shrug his shoulders and dreamily say, "We just sat around the house and watched TV. It was great!" Mario and Samantha had now reached the point where all they needed to enjoy the evening was each other's presence (the fourth stage).

If I am faithful to my daily prayer times and do not lose heart when times get tough, I will eventually find myself in this final stage in the evolution of prayer. This stage is radically different from all the others for two reasons. First, it is not an action like talking or listening, but rather is a state of being. It is not so much what I do during my prayer times, but who I've become because of them. Second, because this is not an action that I can do, it is virtually out of my control. Unlike the other stages, I cannot make this stage happen. It must come as a pure gift from God. All I can do is till the soil so that the land will be fertile when the Sower comes to plant the seeds.

CONCLUSION

Anthony DeMello tells the story of a Hindu disciple asking his master about "enlightenment," which is similar to the experience of this fourth stage. "Master, how can we reach enlightenment?" asked the disciple. "We can no more make enlightenment happen than make the sun rise," was his reply. "Then why do we pray at all?" asked the bewildered disciple. "So that we will be awake when the sun rises," said the master. The growth in my relationship with God is a gift from God. It does not happen because of any effort on my part. My task in prayer, then, is to learn to approach God with open hands, so that God can place his gifts there.

The point of reflecting on the stages of contemplative prayer is *not* so that I may begin progressing on the path. Rather, I reflect on the stages so that I will understand better how God is working in my prayer life. I, for my part, will want to move slowly and take baby steps. Generally speaking, I move into the next level of prayer, *as it feels comfortable to me.* As a matter of fact, I won't be moving anywhere; God will be moving me. He will do so in his own (eternal) time, and sometimes in ways unknown to me. So I should not worry about what stage I'm presently in. I should relax and let God do his mighty work within me.

NOTE

1. This four-stage schema was inspired by a comment made by Gregory I. Carlson, S.J., in *Studies in the Spirituality of Jesuits*, November 1989, p. 5.

chapter three

From Martha to Mary
The Direction of Prayer

The previous chapter presented the evolution of prayer in four stages. But my prayer life can also be spoken of as a life-long process of conversion within me. God saves me through this evolving relationship. But what does God save me from? How will my life change as I grow in my contemplative relationship? And by the end of it, how will I be different from what I am now? This chapter discusses the transformation that will take place within me during the course of my prayer life.

The Human Condition

The following is a recent entry from my prayer-journal:

Dear Lord,

Last week, on Holy Thursday, I was to lead a communion service in the high-security unit of the Suffolk County Jail. After a great deal of preparation, I walked into the big recreation room of the unit and shouted out my weekly invitation, "Prayer services in the multipurpose room." I then walked into the little side room, laid out my stuff and waited. But no one came. After a while, I packed up my stuff and walked out. To leave the unit, I had to walk back through the recreation room where no one had moved from their places in front of the television set. It was painful for me to see that these prisoners were choosing to watch television over coming to my prayer service.

A second painful moment of rejection was just yesterday afternoon. I was to give a presentation on prayer to a group of college students, but only one person showed up and the whole thing was canceled. That was a real humiliation, too.

Sadly, these two rejection moments were a stark reminder to me of who is at the center of my universe, and it's not you, Lord. If it were you, I would not have left that prison licking my own wounds. I may have been disappointed, but I would have been disappointed that the guys chose TV over you, Lord, not over me. Or maybe I wouldn't have been disappointed at all. Perhaps, I would simply have trusted that you were working in their lives in a variety of other ways.

Likewise, if you were really my Lord, I would have talked with the one college student who did show up for that presentation instead of canceling it and walking out of there with my wounded pride. I would have rejoiced in this young woman's wonderful desire to grow closer to you, and I would have done everything in my power to help her to do so. But, unfortunately, I could not see past my own selfish wishes and disappointments.

As I write this journal entry, I sadly wonder if I will ever truly have you as the center of my life. If it does ever happen, it will be because you have made it so, not I. So I realize that even now, after all these years, my prayer is to ask for conversion—my own conversion.

Theologians often use the term "the human condition" to refer to the sinful state of humans from which only God can save. What is it about me that needs redemption? From what am I being saved? How do I become saved? These are all fundamental questions of faith. One could fill a library with the reflections these questions have generated throughout history. Here, I lay out my own reflections and will explore the connection between the human condition and contemplative prayer.

The human condition is such that I spend my life struggling to be my own master and lord. I cling to the illusion that I am the god of my own life, and I go to any lengths to keep that illusion alive. Deep down inside, I know that my own kingship is inadequate, but I cannot accept that. I spend my life trying to prove to others and to myself that I am worthy to be lord. I am obsessed with doing, proving, having, showing, moving, winning, owning and on and on. These actions are my desperate attempts to prove to myself that I am the creator (my products) and the ruler (my control), and am adore-able (my achievements). Because it is a lie, because I am not any of those things, the proof will never be enough. I must constantly engage in more action, make more products, achieve more goals. If I could watch myself from a divine perspective, I'm sure that I would look as silly as a dog chasing his tail.

So what do I do to stop this craziness? How do I put God at the center of my life? Even these simple questions reveal the depth and potency of the human condition, because the questions, themselves, are flawed. They assume that there is something *I* can do to fix the problem. They expose the fact that *I* am still my own savior. I recognize that there is a problem, but I still insist that *I* be the "prime mover," the one doing the fixing.

The truth is that, because of the human condition, I do not have the ability to place God at the center of my life. God will have to place himself there. My job is to stay out of the way and let God do his thing. I need to stop doing and allow God to do the doing to me, in me, for me. My part is so simple, and yet, because I am so stuck in the rut of the human condition, it will take my whole lifetime—maybe more—to completely surrender to God. God will indeed make himself my God, but he will not do so against my free will. He will not push me off the throne. He will patiently, lovingly, slowly take over my life as I awkwardly, painfully, begrudgingly allow him to do so. First, I may allow him to sit on a corner of the throne. After a long while, I will inch over and allow him to sit beside me. Only in the end will I finally sit in my Father's lap and rest there from the childish games of my life.

Even when I become a "good Christian," when I am baptized, pray regularly, and am active in my church, the conversion process is *not* over. The human condition may not have as tight a grip on me, but it is not completely gone. There will still be a very strong part of me that is scrambling for the top. My tactics will change and become more subtle and sophisticated. Instead of blatantly striving for power, position, wealth, I will now conceal this part of me. I will dress it up in an angelic robe. Now, instead of being the best, I will be the holiest. Instead of being the greatest businessman, I will strive to be the greatest minister. Instead of having the most beautiful body, I will build in me the most beautiful soul. Instead of making the most money, I will spend the most on charity. Instead of doing the most for the boss, I will do the most for the Church, the community, the poor, the world. Nothing has changed. I am still the center of my life. It is still all about me: about my (Christian) efforts, my (altruistic) achievements, my (spiritual) beauty. My doggy tail is now purest white, but it is still my doggy tail.

Many Christians never understand or accept this reality. The human condition is too firmly entrenched in their souls. They take too much pride in their Christian actions. Once, at a youth Mass, I noticed someone wearing a T-shirt that said, "I'm not a saint yet, but I'm working on it." What a contradiction in terms! The saints don't work at being saints. *The saints are those who give up!* They are the ones who admit and accept their failure to be holy, and allow God to do holy things within them. They do not "achieve" sainthood; they receive it as a free gift from God. Like Archbishop Romero, they say to God, "I can't. You must." Like Saint Paul, they joyfully proclaim, "I will boast all the more gladly of my weaknesses, so that the power of Christ may dwell in me" (2 Corinthians 12:9).

From Martha to Mary

The Gospel of Luke best reflects this dichotomy between the distorted model of sainthood and the true saint:

> Now as they went on their way, [Jesus] entered a certain village, where a woman named Martha welcomed him into her home. She had a sister named Mary, who sat at the Lord's feet and listened to what he was saying. But Martha was distracted by her many tasks; so she came to him and asked "Lord, do you not care that my sister has left me to do all the work by myself? Tell her then to help me." But the Lord answered her, "Martha, Martha, you are worried and distracted by many things; there is need of only one thing. Mary has chosen the better part, which will not be taken away from her." (Luke 10:38-42)

Many people claim that this passage is about having a balance in one's life between working for the Lord and resting in the Lord.

But that's not really what the passage says, is it? Jesus is quite clear here: "[T]here is need of only one thing. Mary has chosen the better part."

Martha wants to be a disciple, but is obsessed with doing things for Jesus instead of letting Jesus do great things in and through her. Mary represents the person who has surrendered her life to Jesus. She sits at Jesus's feet with nothing to show for herself—no great accomplishments or achievements. She doesn't even have any prepared appetizers to serve him. All she has is her receptive spirit.

Jesus knows well this type of person because his mother, Mary, had the same outlook. She is honored and is the model for all Christians not because of what she did, but because of what she allowed God to do through her. She did not say, "I will do it," but rather, "May it be done to me according to your word" (Luke 1:38, *The New American Bible*).

The problem with the Martha-state is not with actions themselves, of course. Most of the saints lead extremely active lives. The difference lies in what is at the center of one's life. The human condition tempts me to put my actions at the center of my life. In the Martha-state, I work for God, but it is still *my* work that is at the center of my life. Everything is different for the saint. For her, actions are the offspring of God's lordship in her life. They are God's actions being done through her.

The project of my life, then, is to allow God to move me from the Martha-state to the Mary-state—from a life centered on good actions, to a life centered on surrendering to the True King, who does good things within and through me. How do I do that? How do I make surrendering to God my life project? This is where contemplative prayer enters in. When I pray, my goal is to come as close as I can to what Mary did on that day Jesus dropped by for a visit. I sit in stillness with nothing. I sit in God's presence, not proudly presenting products, achievements and accomplishments—Christian or otherwise—but with empty hands. Ultimately, I don't even offer words to God. I am an empty vessel ready to be filled. This is the direction in which I want to go in my contemplative prayer life. It is "the one thing" for which there is need (see Luke 10:42).

What of activities in my prayer, then? Am I to stop praying the rosary, or telling God what's on my mind, or listening to God tell me what's on his mind? No, those activities are still immensely valuable. But in contemplative prayer, they are not ends in themselves. I use those activities to help me get to that quiet Mary-state-of-being and let them go once they get me there.

THE FIRST THING TO SURRENDER

As a beginner, this surrendering begins on day one of my prayer life with the most basic trivialities of prayer: The Lord asks me to surrender my preoccupation with doing prayer perfectly.

Consider these modern-day Marthas and Marys:

Martha: "A few years ago, I was invited to the home of my newly wedded friends. I was told that we would 'hang out' and 'do nothing,' but upon arriving, I found that they took this task of hanging out quite seriously. For instance, everyone knows that the perfect hanging-out activity would be to eat hamburgers in front of the TV. So, three previously unused, natural wood TV trays (given to them as a wedding gift last month) were carefully laid out in the living room, two at the love seat for them and one at the recliner for me. Hamburger patties awaited me at the snack bar accompanied by every possible condiment known to man. Diet drinks were served in jelly-jar glasses (from Crate & Barrel) and there was even an appropriately mindless video ready in the DVD player. There was something about this project of doing nothing that ultimately made me nervous."

Mary: "As a Jesuit novice, I lived in Grand Coteau, Louisiana, a sleepy little Cajun town of about six hundred people. On my evening walks, I loved waving to old Mr. and Mrs. Savoy sitting on their porch and contentedly staring out onto the street at nothing in particular. Since this old couple sat on their porch every evening, one would think that they would have good-looking and comfy chairs to sit in, but that was not the case. Mrs. Savoy's rocker was off-balance and caused the old woman to have a certain skewed look about her, like a picture on a wall that is just crooked enough to make one want to do something about it. The seat of Mr. Savoy's rattan chair had broken long ago and he would have fallen right through if he hadn't stuffed a pillow in the hole. Even with this pillow, he did sink a bit, trapping him so that by the time night fell and the mosquitoes got bad, he could not get up without Mrs. Savoy's assistance. The sagging porch, the slanted old woman, and the trapped old man looked nothing like the glamorous picture of my Martha-like newly wedded friends that sits on my bookshelf at home. And yet, none of these things mattered to the Savoys. The conditions in which they sat never crossed their minds. They just...sat."

As a beginning pray-er I, myself, approached the task of prayer in the same Martha-state that the young newlyweds approached the task of hanging out. I quickly became trapped into a game of Let's Pray! and tried to accomplish the perfect prayer. It was very important for me to do everything correctly in my prayer. I practiced placing my head in the same tilt that the Virgin Mary had in all of those 1950s pictures on the wall of my grandmother's house. I spent a lot of time trying to get into the perfect lotus position, or sitting on one of those little Zen benches. I memorized Latin chants. I read all the right books on prayer, learning the meaning of terms like "kataphatic prayer."

The problem was that I read those books and practiced those positions and techniques in the hope of progressing in prayer. I wanted to know the rules of the road, the policies and procedures, so that I might successfully do prayer. I was approaching prayer in that same frenetic Martha-state that I approached everything in life. Prayer was to be another achievement to be checked off my to-do list—another accomplishment with which I could say (at least to myself), "Look at what I've done. See what a good Christian I'm becoming." I did not realize that prayer must "be done to me" by God.

I, as a beginner, must learn to sit with the Savoys. I must learn from books like this one, not how to sit, but rather how to stop worrying about how to sit. I must not fret about which stage I am in or whether I'm good at praying. All of the little "tips" I find in this book and elsewhere will be of no use to me unless I approach prayer in the spirit of Mary and of the Savoys. Books like these should get me started, not help me finish the job of praying. This is the first moment of surrender. Many more will follow.

CONCLUSION

Have I picked up this book because my prayer seems as sloppy and disheveled as the porch-sitting Savoys? Will I read this book to learn how to "clean it up" and "do it right"? Or will I surrender those preoccupations and let the Lord decide what my prayer should be like? And will I allow this book to teach me to embrace the relationship I already have with God, messy as it might be?

In the previous chapter, I said that the path of contemplative prayer is a path that leads me from Talking at God, through

Talking to God, through Listening to God and finally to Being with God. This four-stage process can be simplified by saying that in contemplative prayer, I move from a Martha-state-of-doing to a Mary-state-of-being. Ultimately, both descriptions come down to an evolution of surrendering to God. This is the direction in which I am going in my journey through prayer. It is the "one thing" necessary.

chapter four

Solitude
A Necessary Tool

If my prayer life can be said to be a journey from the Martha-state to the Mary-state, then solitude can be said to be the vehicle in which I will make this journey. This chapter introduces the concept of solitude, explains how solitude works in contemplative prayer and gives concrete ways to begin practicing solitude.

'Be Still, and Know That I Am God!'[1]

Silence is sometimes defined as "the condition of no sound." Solitude, on the other hand, is a deeper, richer experience. It approaches the experience I have previously referred to as the "Mary-state-of-being" or "Being with God." I can have silence without solitude, but I cannot have solitude without being silent on some level. It is a necessary prerequisite. Most people are uncomfortable with silence, and subconsciously avoid it. But those who long for a state of solitude when they pray must first become accustomed to silence.

Although famous for his anti-Christian philosophy, Friedrich Nietzsche had some interesting insights into human nature. He once said, "When we are alone and quiet, we fear that something will be whispered in our ear. So we hate the silence and drug ourselves with social life." Have you ever noticed how much of our ordinary day is filled with noise and media pollution? Right there in our pockets and purses, we have constant access to the internet, emails, random cat videos, and an endless supply of other useless intrusions. Ever wonder why we are so obsessed with filling the silence in every moment of our day?

Try this. After reading this paragraph, mark your place, put the book down and sit in silence for five minutes. I'll be waiting when you get back...

...Well, how was it? If you're like most people, you probably found that time very awkward and anxiously watched the clock for the five minutes to be up. Nietzsche may be on to something here. For whatever reason, we seem to be afraid of silence.

If I'm only beginning to pray this way, the silence may feel uncomfortable at first. For a while—maybe even a long while—much of my prayer times may be spent simply struggling with the awkwardness of this strange new world of silence. While there are no magic formulas, there are certain techniques that can help me to quiet down. Here are three:

Exercise A: Becoming Aware of My Body

1. I find a sitting position that is comfortable, but not so much so that I will fall asleep easily. A cushioned chair that forces me to sit up straight usually does the trick. In the long run, breathing is easier and more relaxed when I'm sitting up. I sit quietly a few moments, allowing my breathing to slow down and my body to relax.

2. Without moving and in that same quiet state, I focus all of my attention on the big toe of my right foot. I sense the presence of that toe as I never have before. I feel its contentment with simply being there at the end of my foot. In my heart I say to God repeatedly, "Thank you, Lord." After a while, I move on to my entire right foot. I note its peacefulness and tranquility—its lack of anxiety or fear. I say again, "Thank you, Lord."

3. I now allow its partner, the left foot, into the reflection, noting its quietness and thanking God for creating it. I slowly move up from my feet and focus on the solitude of the shins. I continue moving slowly up my body, noting at each stage how peaceful and content each body part is and thanking God for it. I do this exercise very slowly, spending a while at each spot without becoming stuck on any one.

4. When I have reached the top of my head, I pull away slowly and try to get a sense of my entire body as a unified whole at rest and at peace. I go back into my body, very slowly traveling through my various body parts, again observing the stillness that pervades everywhere. I now pull away again and revisit the quietness of my entire body.

5. I spend a few minutes soaking in that quiet state.

Exercise B: The Mantra

The word *mantra* means "quieting the mind." It is a sacred word or phrase repeated several times over in order to quiet oneself and become focused on God. Here's how to do it:

1. I find a comfortable sitting position as described in the previous exercise. I sit quietly a few moments, allowing my breathing to slow down and my body to relax.

2. I close my eyes and begin to focus all of my attention on my breathing in and out. Many spiritual guides say, "Become aware of your breathing," because most of the time I don't even notice it. I observe it as though I were a scientist who has just discovered to his astonishment the strange and wondrous act of respiration. I note that as I further relax, my breathing gets slower, quieter.

3. I choose a word or short phrase that expresses my desire for God to be present. Some of my favorite mantras are "Jesus," *"Maranatha"* (or its English translation, "Come, Lord Jesus"[2]), and "My Lord, My God."[3] I also like using Saint John Paul II's motto, *"Totus Tuus,"* which is Latin for "totally yours." I begin to call on God by slowly and reverently repeating my mantra over and over in my mind.

4. I notice that my mantra is gradually coming in sync with my breathing. Using the word, *Jesus* for instance, as I inhale, I say the syllable, "Jee," and as I exhale I say, "sus."

5. I continue this practice for several minutes. Over time (and it does take time), I will notice myself reaching a state of quiet.

EXERCISE C: CHANTING

1. I sit and breathe in the way described in the previous exercise.

2. I begin chanting some quiet, slow and simple religious song. The songs of Taizé are great for this exercise. But there may also be the refrain from some song I've heard at church on Sunday or that I sang as a little child. I may even want to make up a song using the words of my mantra. For example, I like to sing, "Praise God, praise God," over and over again to the tune of *Amazing Grace*. The point is to use a song whose words are so simple that it requires little mental effort to sing it.

3. I sing it over and over, allowing it to "take over my body" so that I sense every part of me floating along the gentle waves of the song.

4. If inclined to do so, I allow the stillness to let even the song drift away.

I must not use these exercises as though they were magic formulas. I cannot conjure up solitude with a spell. These exercises are merely techniques to slow myself down and to help me to narrow my focus to God. Because there is no magic here, I will need to experiment in order to custom fit them for myself. These exercises are not mutually exclusive. I can combine one with another in any way I like. The point of these exercises is to become relaxed and still, so I should not turn them into tasks that I need to accomplish. Instead, I surrender control and let my body take me to this place called "stillness." My body knows how to get there; all I have to do is let it drive.

I may have the problem of being preoccupied with time. If I am not yet used to silence, it may seem like a very long stretch. I may go mad trying to keep myself from peeking at the clock. If this problem persists, I can try these tips:

- I decrease my prayer time. If I am praying for twenty minutes and am becoming frustrated with how long this time seems, I can do three five-minute blocks of time for awhile. Later, I change it to two ten-minute blocks, then one fifteen-minute block and finally back to twenty minutes.

- I set my alarm for the time period I plan to pray and then move my watch or clock out of sight. That way I won't be tempted to peek.

- I make the discomfort a prayer to God. I ask God to accept my resolve to sit in the uncomfortable stillness as a sign of my commitment to grow closer to him.

Learning to reach this state of quiet is a very gradual process and will break down only if I try to rush it. (Note: I was not really able to enjoy this until after an entire year of trying.) I must remember that to reach *for* God is to reach God. (See "One last thing before beginning…," Chapter One, page 10.) Merely attempting to place myself in the quietness of God will fill my life with God's presence in ways I've never dreamed.

Solitude: a definition

The last segment of the Aunt Sally story in Chapter Two described precious memories of the two of us loving each other through a mysterious experience of silence. Have you ever loved and been loved by someone so much that you found yourselves sitting in silence for long periods without ever feeling uncomfortable? Now here's the really big question: Have you and God ever had such closeness?

That closeness is what I strive for in my contemplative prayer life. It is that Mary-state-of-being, whereby God and I sit together with nothing in our hands. I am not *saying* any prayers such as the rosary or the Lord's Prayer. I am not speaking spontaneously to myself or to God. Nor am I even *listening* to some message from God. God and I are in a transcendent state wherein there is no action at all, only being. And in this state of being there is a oneness in which there are no clear distinctions between "I" and God.

These extraordinary moments are rare. They can neither be created by me, nor even predicted by me. They come and go as they will. No, they do not come and go; they just happen with no entrance and no exit. It is a mysterious and powerful experience of the wild, roaming Holy Spirit of God. That is why I wrote in Chapter Two that, while I can work on the first three stages, I cannot make this one happen. It must be given to me as a pure, unannounced and unmerited gift from God. I like to think of these moments as appetizers from the Heavenly Banquet because they give me a taste of the indescribable experience of the next life.

As I said in the Aunt Sally chapter, what I *can* do is prepare the soil for the Sower. Or, put another way, I can work on emptying the cup that is my soul so that God may come and fill it with himself. This emptying is what I call solitude. It is not the gift of the state of being, but it is the ultimate disposition for receiving that gift.

FEELING FOR AN OPENING

If you ever get the opportunity
to keep your mouth shut,
don't pass it up.[4]

Because solitude is that place where the transcendent and the ordinary come together, it, too, is not fully under my control. While I can lean toward solitude, I cannot force my way into it. I must wait quietly and patiently at its edges, "feeling" for an opening. When I find such an opening, I can then drift into it. In the same way, if after a while, I feel myself coming out of solitude, I cannot force my way back in. Any such exertion will bring me out of it that much more quickly. I must let the flow of my prayer carry me where it will.

When I speak of this topic to groups, many of those listening return blank stares. One brave soul eventually raises his hand and says, "Yeah, that's nice. But how do you actually do it?" So let me be as concrete as possible here. This is how my own prayer usually goes:

• I wake up early in the morning, put on my favorite robe and stumble down to the kitchen to make a pot of coffee. Reverently carrying a full cup of java, I return to my prayer chair in my room. I note the time (so that I don't have to worry about it during prayer). I check to see that all of my stuff of prayer is ready at my side: I have my Bible open to a passage I might want to pray over. I have a pen stuck in my journal at the place where I left off. I have my rosary, my prayer books, my spiritual reading—the whole shebang—sitting there on the end table next to my armchair.

- While contentedly sipping my coffee, I begin to take notice of God's presence in the room. It's not as if a fiery ball suddenly appears—God is already present, remember? It's just that I'm coming to a conscious awareness of who is already there. Remembering that I am to lean into solitude, I put my cup down and adjust my sitting position so that my back is straight and my body is comfortable, and I close my eyes. Perhaps I will begin saying a mantra in my mind over and over again, "Come, Lord Jesus... Come, Lord Jesus...," or maybe I will slowly, silently sing to myself a simple song with very few words.

- All the while, I am feeling for an opening in the solitude. I am allowing myself, as much as possible, to slip into a prayerful stillness. Maybe my mantra or song will slip away. Maybe it won't. It doesn't matter to me; it can do what it wills.

- If I am in a state of solitude, I will know it by the indescribable feeling of peace and serenity it brings. There is no chair now, no room, no Bible, no person called "me." There is only God. I am there, too. But my soul has returned home, deep inside God. I do not know where in God my soul is. I do not care. All there is, is God.

- Or maybe none of that will happen. Maybe I won't find an opening into solitude. Maybe I'll feel only the cloth of my robe on my sunburned shoulders. Maybe the mosquito bite on my foot will itch. Maybe I'll find myself drumming my fingers to the beat of my roommate's shower-singing rendition of "Yesterday" in the bathroom down the hall. No problem. The Lord and I will join the band. The solitude is great and I will enter into it whenever possible, but I won't worry about it if it doesn't come. The two of us will do something else. As long as we're spending time together, it doesn't make all that much difference what we're doing.

- So, if after a while I do not find myself in solitude, I may slowly, quietly begin whatever activity I sense the Lord is in the mood for. How do I know what he is in the mood for? Well, since we are one in prayer, his mood and my mood are the same. This was one of Saint Ignatius' greatest insights. He said that one of the strongest indicators of God's will is the person's own desires in prayer.[5] The trick is to check my moods *after* I've spent some time in silence. Many times I will begin my prayer time with some particular activity in mind. There may be a great Bible passage I want to reflect on, for instance. But once in the prayer, I don't sense a movement that way. Maybe, some other Bible passage or some whole new activity will come up instead.

- Even if the solitude doesn't happen, I will often just sit quietly with my mantra or my simple chant. Whatever I choose to do, I will do it very slowly and quietly. I will pause from time to time, close my eyes and be still again. I am once again feeling for an opening into solitude. Maybe I will slip into it this time, but only for a few brief minutes, and then I will find myself out of it again. No problem. I'll move back to something else. And my prayer goes on this way, fluctuating from quiet prayer activity, to greater quiet, to solitude, to my activity again.

Each and every prayer time has its own unique rhythm. I may spend practically the entire time in the solitude or no time at all there. Or I may have some unique combination of activity and solitude. While always leaning toward solitude, I will, at each moment, embrace the gift of God's presence in whatever form God chooses just then. Have you ever watched two young lovers sitting on the couch playfully toying with each other's fingers? True, it makes everyone else in the room gag, but how wonderful it is that their love can make them so unselfconscious. In similar fashion, I sometimes sort of forget what I'm doing when I pray because my focus is on God rather than the activity itself. This unselfconsciousness frees me from the obsessive speculations about "What state am I in right now?" It doesn't matter. Wherever I am, the Lord is here with me.

It's Sort of Like…

The whole experience can be likened to the image of a scuba diver in the ocean. Instead of swimming on his own, he is lowered down and hoisted up by a rope that runs from

his suit to the surface above. The scuba diver loves to dive as deeply as possible, so he will go as far down as the rope will allow. On some days, the rope allows him to spend the whole time on the bottom. On other days, the rope is so short that he spends his whole time floating on the surface. On still other days, he finds himself bobbing up and down from the ocean floor to the surface. The moments he spends down on the bottom are the most precious to him, but he is not sad or angry when the rope doesn't allow him down that far. He loves diving so much that it doesn't matter much to him how far down he is at any given moment. Each depth of the ocean has its own life and adventure. Whatever depth he finds himself in he thoroughly enjoys. He will play and explore there until he notices that the rope has more give to it, allowing him the opportunity of going deeper. So, down he goes. Or maybe he will notice the rope gently tugging him back to the surface. No matter: He'll enjoy any level.

In prayer, *I lean into being* and away from activity. If I am doing some prayerful activity and notice my spirit beginning to get quieter, I'll put whatever I'm doing down and let myself slowly sink. Otherwise, I'll enjoy the prayer activity I have in front of me at the moment. I may even find myself on the surface for the entire time. It won't feel as though this prayer time is very deep at all. Instead, it will be filled with silly distractions and useless thoughts. Even this is no problem. I'll find the Lord floating among the rubber duckies, too.

Conclusion

In the previous chapter I said that my objective in prayer is to allow God to move me from the Martha-state of doing to the Mary-state of receptivity. In this chapter, I have said that the way to get to that Mary-state is through solitude—through leaning into being. So whatever I am doing in any given prayer—whether it be listening for God's voice, or speaking spontaneously to God or simply praying ready-made prayer—I am always in the process of allowing God, if it is his will, to take me into the depths where there is only God and I. This is the mark of contemplative prayer.

Notes

1. Psalm 46:10.
2. Revelation 22:20.
3. See John 20:28.
4. This advice is a paraphrase of a line from Robert N. Peck's *A Day No Pigs Would Die* (New York: Random House, 1994).
5. *SpirEx*, 175.

STAGE ONE—TALKING AT GOD
Ready-made Prayer

In these next three chapters, I return to the stages introduced in Chapter Two, spending a chapter on each of the first three stages. I begin with stage one, Talking at God.

PRAYERS 'OFF-THE-RACK'

Talking at God is the stage wherein I use prayers or sets of prayers that someone else has written. C.S. Lewis called this type of prayer, "ready-made prayer." It is also referred to as traditional prayer, common prayer or written prayer. Now, why would I want to pray this way? If God loves me personally, why would I not want to speak to him in my own words?

First, I may want to use ready-made prayers because:

- *They're great.* They are written beautifully and express what I'm feeling right now.

- *They connect me with the eternal Church.* When I pray the Hail Mary, for example, I join with all Christians who have prayed that prayer since the twelfth century.

- *They connect me with the universal Church.* The Lord's Prayer, for example, is the only prayer that practically all Christians pray. It is a great way to be spiritually united with the almost two billion Christians around the world.

- *They connect me with me.* Like good ritual, they interconnect my past with my present and future, the ordinary with the transcendent and the reality with the ideal.

Second, I may not be able to pray in my own words right now because:

- *I don't know what to say.* For whatever reason, I just can't put into words how I'm feeling or what I want to say to God right now. At times, I want to express my love for God, but I don't have anything in particular to say.

- *I'm distracted.* For example, I may be driving to work, exercising, traveling or waiting in a long line. These are fantastic times to pray, but I can't concentrate enough to do any deep prayer. By using a prayer I know by heart and can say effortlessly, I can continue doing whatever task is at hand.

- *I'm emotionally distracted.* If I'm feeling some strong emotion like anxiety, fury or fear, I may have trouble settling down enough for the other types of prayer. I could even have trouble settling down when I'm really thrilled about something or am overcome by some happy emotion. There are ready-made prayers for every occasion. I can lament with the psalmist who says, "Why are you cast down, O my soul?" (Psalm 42:5). Or I can joyfully belt out an amazing *Amazing Grace*.

- *I'm tired.* Sometimes I am too exhausted to pray deeply. I use these ready-made prayers to communicate the words that I'm too tired to think of myself.

FIVE WAYS TO PRAY READY-MADE PRAYERS
The First Way: Reflecting on the Words

Part of the reason that these prayers are passed on from one person to another is that they touch some spiritual cord deep within the soul. The words aptly express some deep sentiment that I can't always understand or articulate. So, obviously, one way to pray these prayers is to reflect on their words as I am saying or singing them.

Many times, prayers that I have said all my life lose their meaning. I don't even listen to the words anymore. Simply paying attention to the words I've always recited but haven't always prayed could renew my prayer life. For example, when I say, "... and forgive us our trespasses," am I even aware of what trespasses I have committed lately? Am I truly sorry for them? Do I really believe that God desires to forgive them? And when I say "as we forgive those..." am I cognizant of who has hurt me lately? Am I really ready to forgive them? These two phrases alone are pregnant with spiritual implications. At the least, they assume (a) a great deal of faith in God, (b) some serious soul-searching and (c) a willingness to make difficult changes in my life. If I really reflected on each part of the Lord's Prayer every day, what an amazing transformation might take place within me!

EXERCISE D: REFLECTING ON THE LORD'S PRAYER

1. I pray the Lord's Prayer slowly and reverently three times.

2. I choose one phrase within the prayer to reflect on. I ask myself, "Who is God in this phrase?" For example, in the phrase, "Give us this day our daily bread," my answer might be "God is provider." If so, then what does God provide? Why does he provide it? How much does he provide? When does he provide? Or in the phrase, "Your kingdom come," I might say, "God is king." If so, what kind of a king is he? What would it be like if his kingdom came? Or has it already come? And if so, how? How has it not? Why has it not?

3. I go back over the phrase, asking myself, "Who am I in this phrase?" In the daily bread phrase, I might say, "I am hungry." If so, then what am I hungry for? Why am I hungry? How will I be fed? In the kingdom phrase, I might say, "I am God's subject." If so, then what does my King expect of me? What do I expect of my King? How far will I go in service to him? How loyal am I? How loyal do I want to be? What other kings am I tempted to serve?

4. Some phrases will work better than others. I use the ones that work and skip the ones that don't. I take as much or little time as I want with any given phrase. If things are going really well, perhaps I will want to dedicate a whole prayer time to just one phrase that is meaningful to me.

The Second Way: When Soul-searching Isn't Possible

On the other hand, I sometimes choose to pray ready-made prayers specifically because I cannot do the sort of soul searching required in other types of prayer. As mentioned earlier, sometimes I'm too tired, distracted, upset or confused to do that type of reflection. I do want to be reconciled with God and my community, but, because it's 1:00 A.M. and I've had a very long day, I will fall asleep the moment I start reflecting on just who did what to whom. So I pray "...and forgive us our trespasses, as we forgive those who trespass against us," as a way of expressing my sincere desire for repentance and reconciliation and my true hope that God will help me sort out all of the details after I get a good night's rest. Even though I have not reflected on the words, I have certainly prayed a beautiful and sincere prayer.

EXERCISE E: WHEN I'M UPSET

1. I pray the rosary. Working through the various beads and their corresponding prayers is a simple project that can take my mind

off my problems for a few minutes.

2. If my anxiety, anger, fear or hurt persists throughout the rosary, distracting me from the words, I don't worry about it. As I pray, I imagine being held by Mother Mary who is praying to God for me and with me.

3. Using my imagination, I try to get a picture of that spot on my soul that is angry, hurt or whatever. I imagine my spoken words anointing that tender spot, soothing it like a cool balm on a painful sunburn.

The Third Way: Linking Myself to the Past

A third way to pray ready-made prayers is to allow the prayers to link myself with the past and/or with others who have prayed this particular prayer throughout the years. Doing so may allow me to bridge across rifts between myself and my past or between my Church and other Churches. The exercises below show what I mean by this.

EXERCISE F: LINKING THE MANY ME'S:

1. I choose a prayer that I have prayed since childhood and throughout my life.

2. I pray it aloud very slowly and reverently, as I might imagine cloistered monks do.

3. I pray it a second time, imagining all of the me's of my past standing before God, praying it together in one voice. I pray with the happy six-year-old Mark, the awkward fifteen-year-old Mark, the idealistic eighteen-year-old Mark and so on. I might pray it over and over again, each time bringing in a new (old) me from the past.

4. I pray it another time, imagining this motley crew being joined by future me's (a fifty-year-old me, a seventy-year-old me and so on) all fervently praying this prayer, each with his own motivations, dreams and failures. I imagine that, despite the diversity within the many me's, my prayerful voices are in perfect unison as they reach out to God.

5. I pray it another time, imagining the me's slowly merging into one another. As this happens, I keep praying the prayer, but slow it down as the me's merge.

6. I keep slowing down the prayer and imagining the merging until there is only one me praying softly. I allow the prayer to quietly slip away and allow myself some time in the stillness.

EXERCISE G: LINKING MY PRAYER TO OTHERS'

1. I find a psalm that fits my mood. If I'm feeling grateful for God's providence, for instance, I could use Psalm 139. Or I could just use the psalm I heard at Mass last Sunday.1

2. I pray it aloud very slowly and reverently, as I might imagine cloistered monks do.

3. I pray it a second time, imagining all of the people alive today who have at one time or another prayed this same psalm. I imagine this massive flock of worshipers standing before God, praying it in unison.

4. I pray it a third time, imagining this flock being multiplied by all the people throughout history, Jews and Christians alike, who have fervently prayed this psalm. I imagine this unified resounding voice rising to God.

5. I go through the same merging process as in the exercise above, allowing the prayer to come down to one small voice—mine—drifting into nothingness.

The Fourth Way: Singing

Not many people think of song as prayer, but St. Augustine said that to sing is to pray twice. It's a good idea to start collecting prayerful music. Instrumental music, nature sounds and collections of Christian songs that are very simple and easy to learn work best. It's good to store a couple of the songs in my head so that I can call them forth at will.

EXERCISE H: MAKING A JOYFUL NOISE

1. I do Exercise C of Chapter Four. I ride those prayerful waves for a while.

2. I may use *Amazing Grace* since I know the first verse by heart. After a while, I sense in myself a need to ask God to draw closer to me. So I change the words a little to fit how I feel at the present time. I may change the words of *Amazing Grace* to simply, "Come near, come near, come near." I sing the entire song using only those two words, and I sing it slowly and quietly enough to sense God's presence coming nearer. Or maybe I will sense in myself a need to worship and adore God. I may change the words to, "Praise God, praise God, praise God."

3. If I feel myself getting quieter and quieter, I let myself go. Instead of singing the two words, I might slowly drift into a very soft humming of the song.

4. I may feel myself going even deeper. The song will drop away altogether. Only God and I are left.

The Fifth Way: The Mantra

The fifth way to pray ready-made prayers is to use them as a sort of mantra, a word or phrase repeated slowly and reverently in an effort to still my mind in order to center all of my attention on God.

EXERCISE I: THE ROSARY AS MANTRA

1. I review how a mantra is normally used by looking back to Exercise B of Chapter Four.

2. Instead of using the short word or phrase, I pray the rosary, using that same mantra rhythm. I recite the prayers in a sort of slow cadence. It should sound like an auctioneer in slow motion or the guttural chanting of Tibetan monks. At first, it will sound strange to me, but after a while, I'll get used to it.

3. Once I've got a steady rhythm going, I imagine myself floating on the sound waves. I imagine that I am floating deeper and deeper into God. I gently float along those waves, until I lose myself therein. I don't worry about where I am in the rosary at this point. I can always return to it later if it drops away.

LEAN INTO BEING

I must remember that my overall objective is not necessarily to accomplish a whole rosary or an entire psalm. Prayer is neither a competition with myself, nor an assignment from God. In contemplative prayer, my objective is to drift as close as I can to the Mary-state-of-being. Every prayer exercise and activity I do is to be used as a vehicle to get me to that place of quiet. If I sense myself drifting to that ocean floor,2 I let myself go.

For each exercise above, I move very slowly and quietly. Throughout my prayer time, I should be constantly feeling for an opening into the solitude. The deeper down I drift, the less important the prayer activity becomes. I can drop the activity altogether if I feel so inclined.

In Exercise H above, for example, I go from singing *Amazing Grace* with the real words of verse one, to singing it with only two or three words (for example, "come near"), to merely humming it quietly, to dropping it altogether. I may stay on that ocean floor for the rest of the prayer time and never return to the song. Or, my time on the bottom may be very brief and I may sense myself drifting up again. If so, I pick up the song again at any level I please. There is no rigid procedure here. I lean into the deeper levels, but only insofar as it feels natural to me.

THINGS TO AVOID

There are three pitfalls of this type of prayer that need to be kept in mind. First, I shouldn't allow the prayers to become so mechanical that they no longer mean anything to me. Sometimes I'm inclined to pray ready-made prayers merely to fulfill my obligation to pray. (Remember the silly games I spoke of in Chapter One.) If this is my operative mindset about prayer, then my relationship with God will never grow.

Second, I must not fall into the trap of thinking that there is some magic to these prayers. God is not keeping score of my prayer, checking to make sure that I have prayed exactly *ten* Hail Mary's in each decade and ready to disqualify me if I lose count. These notions are superstitious and have no place in a Christian prayer life. The purpose of the particularities of the prayers (for example, five decades in a rosary, nine days in a novena and so on) is to allow the Church to pray in unison. There is no magic in the format.

Third, I must beware of the Martha syndrome. Ready-made prayers have the unfortunate potential to make me achievement oriented. I can grow prideful about the nine-day novena that I *accomplished* or can feel guilty about innocently falling asleep in the middle of the rosary. This mindset keeps me—rather than God—at the center of my prayer life.

CONCLUSION

One of the best things about ready-made prayers is that their ritual nature instills in me a sense of unity and continuity. They unite my particular prayer time to prayers and pray-ers of all time. Because they require little creative concentration on my part, they allow me to pray at times when all other forms of prayer would be too demanding of my attention. Whether I actually reflect on the words of the prayer or simply allow the rhythm to carry me to a sacred space, ready-made prayers will always play a vital role in my prayer life.

NOTES

1. See the appendices for suggestions of Scripture passages, apps, and other recourses.

2. See "It's sort of like..." in Chapter Four, page 48.

STAGE ONE: TALKING AT GOD

- *It is sometimes referred to as:* ready-made prayer, common prayer, written prayer, or traditional prayer.

- *Basically it is*: reciting a prayer or set of prayers written by someone else.

- *Some examples include:* the Lord's Prayer, the rosary, the Liturgy of the Hours.

- *The advantages of this type of prayer are*: It is easy to do; it links me with others; it has the qualities of ritual (see "The

Value of Ritual" in Chapter One, page 5); it can be used as a mantra; it expresses what I can't at the moment.

- *The limitation of this type of prayer is:* It does not necessarily foster a personal relationship with God.

- *The distortions of this type of prayer are:* I can make it a superstitious act; I can get bored with it; it can become mechanical to me—I can recite it without putting my heart into it; I can get stuck in the rut of "accomplishing prayer."

- *The transition to the next level might come when:* I want a more personal type of prayer.

chapter six

Stage Two—Talking to God
Extemporaneous Prayer

When I was ten years old, my family moved out of the little wood frame house in which I grew up and into a new and bigger house that Mom and Dad built in the country. Although the house was only about a mile away from our old house, the move was an enormous one for me. It was filled with adventure, intrigue, and danger. One evening, several months after the move, I found myself terribly upset about never being able to live in the old house again. I was so homesick! As luck would have it, my mother was out of town that weekend and my father was out for the evening. I was too ashamed to cry in front of my older brother who was in his room listening to music.

After I spent an eternity (probably only an hour or so) pacing all around the house, my dad finally came home. I did not let him settle into his recliner too long before I bashfully approached him and said, "Daddy, I'm real sad."

"What's wrong?" he asked.

As big fat tears welled up in my eyes, and with quivering voice, I said, "I miss the little house." Then my pipes burst and I was crying up a storm.

Dad gently scooped me up, sat me in his lap and held me for a while. After allowing me a few moments of crying, he said, "Tell me all the things you loved about our little house."

I told him everything. I told him how much I used to love climbing up the china-ball tree in the backyard and gathering the china-balls as ammo for the upcoming battle with my brothers. I told him how much I loved playing in the "Cabo'n," (what we Cajuns call the little tool shed behind our house). And I told him of my daily visits with Mrs. Lou Wilda, our next-door neighbor, and how when I had finished reading every last one of her children's books from the bookshelf in her living room, she congratulated me by letting me choose one to take home—for keeps!

When I had exhausted myself with all my stories, Dad let me sit there a moment in the quiet of my memories. Then he said, "Now, tell me all about the stuff you love about this house."

Off I went again! I told him all about how much I loved the many rooms in which to play hide and seek. I told him about all the fun my friend and I had playing on Dad's farm equipment parked in the field behind the house. (Dad showed tremendous self-restraint at this point!) I told him that I had a new friend who lived down the road and how he took me all through the woods behind his house and showed me some of his secret hideaways.

When I again exhausted myself, I quieted down and just let Dad rock me awhile in the recliner. I don't remember if he said anything as we rocked. All I remember is that by the time he took me to bed, I had already begun my descent into peaceful sleep.

There is very little that needs to be said about this stage. It is beautiful in its simplicity. Talking to God is simply the stage wherein I go beyond prayers written by someone else and pray in my own words. I simply tell God whatever is on my mind, rattling on as long as I want, about whatever I want, telling him my stories like a little boy sitting in his father's lap.

In this stage, I can talk to God as I would a trusted friend, a parent or a spouse. I can speak to God in whatever way I like: through talking aloud, through my imagination or through writing it out. To say that I go beyond ready-made prayer is not to say that I drop that type of prayer altogether. One type of prayer does not preclude another. They complement and enrich one another. This is not like a little girl who abandons her tricycle for her new bicycle. The girl does so because the tricycle is obsolete. That will never be true about these various types of prayer. All of them will continue to play a vital role in my prayer life.

Many people are hesitant to pray spontaneously because they feel a little silly talking to someone who doesn't talk back. They don't have that sense of dialogue with God that they have in everyday conversation. But, in a way, that one-sidedness is a good thing. I once belonged to a group that met occasionally to do faith sharing. We simply sat in a circle and, one at a time, told the group what was currently happening in our lives. For ten or fifteen minutes, I was allowed to say to this group whatever I felt like saying. All in the group simply listened quietly. Occasionally, someone would ask a question for clarification, but otherwise they would not respond to what I said. They just listened. I've been in similar groups that had a more dialogical format, whereby the members of the group would respond and react to whatever I said. One might think that this second format would be much more beneficial, and it's true that having a dialogue about current issues in my life was a great thing. But the first way had advantages of its own. In that group, I could say whatever I wanted and did not have to worry about how others would react. At times, I don't want, need or can't accept feedback from others. I just need someone to listen to me. I just need to get it out. That is what is great about God's role in this type of prayer. God just listens without some hidden agenda of his own or prejudgments about the topic at hand or about me. Sometimes God just listens because he knows that, right now, that is what I need most.

COMFORT LEVELS WITH GOD

When, as a high school teacher, I would ask a student what it was he liked about his newfound love, he would often say, "She's really great to talk to. I feel like I can tell her anything." This is the beautiful feeling I get when I pray spontaneously to God. To pray in this way usually implies that God and I have reached a deeper level in our loving relationship.

As people grow into adulthood they learn how to edit everything that they speak aloud and to censor statements that might cause problems. Typical adults have an uncanny ability to evaluate everything they say before they say it. While conversing with anyone, they (consciously or subconsciously) rigorously "inspect" each statement before speaking it aloud, asking themselves: Is this statement:

appropriate?

logical?

related to the topic?

safe to say to this person?

persuasive?

too cerebral or too simplistic?

And on and on. This is not necessarily a bad thing. In fact, the complete absence of the censure mechanism is a sign of a psychological problem. On the other hand, the more I must censor myself in any given conversation, the less comfortable I feel and the less emotionally satisfying is the conversation. In a way, one could define a friend as someone with whom I have the fewest restrictions when I speak. I can say whatever is on my mind and know that even if it is inappropriate, stupid or irrelevant, my friend will not reject me, scorn me or mock me.

A tragic irony of prayer is that many people censure themselves with God more than with anyone else. Many people feel they need to say just the right thing to God in order to keep God happy, or at least in order to hold back his wrath. They do not believe that God loves them unconditionally and will accept anything they say. Those who flourish in this type of prayer are those who can peel away these layers of censorship. Consequently, they find this type of prayer a freeing experience.

How to Pray in This Way

As mentioned before, this stage is beautiful in its utter simplicity. Once I get over the initially strange feeling of speaking in a monologue, there are few complications. To pray in this stage, I simply talk to God as I would a close friend or a beloved parent. I say, "Good morning, Lord. It's great to be alive today. Lately, I've been feeling so grateful for all of the gifts you've given me, especially for the gift of my family...." Or the prayer may go something like this: "Lord, I'm so angry today. I can't believe the boss is still on my case about that screw-up the other day. Why can't he just get off my back?..." Or even, "God, are you really up there? I've been praying to you faithfully all this time, and you never seem to give me any sign that you're listening or are even there...."

Some of the things I bring up with God might include:

- my predominant emotions

- my concrete efforts (successful or not) to serve God lately

- my desires, hopes, fear or anxieties about the future

- my commitment to serve God in a new and deeper way

- my best and worst moments of the day

- my problems with being Christian and my faith struggles

- my addictions to my smart phone, to food, to that third beer, to grumpiness, and so on.

- my unresolved issues of the past
- my gratitude for all the gifts that God has given me
- the person on my mind right now

Lean into Being

Looking back on the story at the beginning of this chapter, it is clear to see what it is that finally allowed me to descend into peaceful sleep. It was not because of anything my dad said, but because of the experience of getting it all out of my system. As a pastoral counselor, I am often struck by the physical transformation a person experiences after finally sharing what has been troubling him or her. Before the story, the person sits stiffly in the chair—every muscle tense and taut, and the emotional blockage is apparent on his or her face. After the story, the shoulders drop and every part of the person seems to unravel peacefully in the chair.

That is what happens when I pray extemporaneously. After choking up whatever it is I am anxious, excited, nervous, thrilled, or angry about, I can then relax as my Heavenly Father rocks me into stillness.

So it doesn't matter what I say, how long I speak, or what words I use. Nor does it matter whether I speak it aloud or only in my heart. All that is important is that I let myself get it all out without any censorship of words or feelings. So long as it is a true expression of who I am today, it is a beautiful prayer. When I am finished saying all that I have to say, I can simply rest in quiet and peaceful exhaustion. In this way I allow myself to lean into being.

Prayer through Journaling

More will be said of journaling in Chapter Ten. For now, suffice it to say that a prayer journal is a like a diary of the spiritual movements of my life. I can use the journal itself as an instrument of prayer. I begin my prayer time with the solitude exercises found in Chapter Four. Then when my spirit is quiet and peaceful, I start writing in a sort of stream-of-consciousness way—without thinking about it or censoring, I write the first things that come to mind.

I like to begin every journal entry with "Dear God" to remind myself that this is not merely an introspective reflection but a prayer to my Creator and Father.

If I like, I can choose some particular topic to write about. Here are a few examples:

- my deepest desire

- my greatest fear

- a relationship in my life that I wish were stronger

- my biggest confusion

- the person I really want to be

- my biggest sin

- my most common little sin

- my unhealthy attachments or addictions

- the gifts God has given me

- the people I love and who love me

- what I want written on my tombstone and why

- the things I forget to be grateful for

- the "me" that nobody knows about

Speaking and journaling are only two ways to express these sentiments. There are many others. I may want to communicate with

God by writing a poem, drawing a picture or even doing some bodily action like bowing, kneeling or even dancing.

Exercise J: Drawing God and me

Before beginning this prayer, I set out a blank sheet of paper and a bunch of colored pencils.

1. I begin prayer with the solitude exercises of Chapter Four.

2. After spending a while in stillness, I pick up a pencil and write at the top of the sheet of paper, "God and me." Then, remaining quiet and relaxed, I draw a picture of the two of us—choosing images (persons, animals or objects) to represent God and me. I do not stop to think about how I should portray God or how I want myself to appear. I just draw.

3. After I am finished, I put the pencils down and try to descend back into the stillness.

4. After a while, I spend some time discussing what I have drawn with God. Why have I chosen that particular color for God? What is the image I have chosen for God? A father? A storm? A tree? Why have I chosen that image? What image have I chosen for me and why? In the picture, where am I in relation to God and why? Is there anything else in the picture? Why did I include this?

5. After telling God all about my picture, I again spend a little time in the stillness of my prayer.

A TIME TO HEAL

The following is an exercise that may help to heal some past wounds. It is a potentially painful exercise and should not be taken lightly. I will probably need to pray this exercise many times before a lasting healing can take place.

Exercise K: Meeting a younger me

1. I do Exercise C of Chapter Four. I ride those prayerful waves for a while.

2. I imagine that sitting in an empty chair across from me is a

me from my past. I choose some difficult period in my life when I was troubled, anxious, angry, traumatized or was experiencing some serious problem.

3. I speak tenderly to that troubled me, showing him my present perception of his problem. I might want to express forgiveness of my younger me for the mistakes he made, or comfort him and tell him that he's going to be OK. Or I may not be ready for such gentleness yet. I may need to yell at him or scold him right now. There is only one rule here: I should be honest and should not censor myself.

4. When I have said all that has come to mind, I relax every part of me and allow the quiet of my prayer to take over.

5. Regardless of what I say to him, I see him off by telling him that I love him (...provided that I do love him. If not, I tell him the most loving thing that I can muster up right now.).

6. Once my younger me leaves the room, I notice Jesus now sitting in that chair. I tell him everything I'm feeling about the conversation I just had. Again, I allow myself to say whatever comes to mind without worrying about how Jesus will respond.

7. I again relax into the stillness. Perhaps I will go back to the quiet simple song with which I began the prayer time. I sit in the stillness and silence for as long as I can.

CONCLUSION

My need for "spilling my guts" is as strong now as it was when I was ten. And like my earthly father, my Heavenly Father eagerly pulls me close to him and says to me, "Tell me all about it."

TALKING TO GOD

- *It is sometimes referred to as:* extemporaneous prayer, spontaneous prayer, "telling God what's on my mind and in my heart."

- *Basically it is:* talking (aloud or in my imagination) to God as I would a friend, parent or teacher.

- *Some examples include:* "Hey, God. It's me, Mark. I had a really great day, today...."; "Dear God, I just can't figure out how to fix my problem with...."

- *The advantages of this type of prayer are:* It is personal and informal; it is fairly easy to do and can be done at any time; it allows me to vent thoughts and feelings that need to be expressed.

- *The limitations of this type of prayer are:* It is not a dialogue, so it feels a little strange—as if I'm talking to myself.

- *The transition to the next level might come when:* I want to hear God's response. I want his feedback, advice, affirmation and so on.

chapter seven

STAGE THREE—LISTENING TO GOD
Meditative Prayer

Many times, when I ask someone, "How do you pray?" the response will be, "I just tell Jesus what's on my mind and speak to him from my heart." I sometimes ask such a person, "And how does Jesus respond?" This question often comes as a surprise. He or she has never expected (and therefore never listened for) a response from God.

An important step in my prayer life is when I move from Talking at God and Talking to God to Listening to God. The Lord will never tire of hearing my voice and always takes great delight in listening to my story. On the other hand, God has many important things to say to me and is waiting for the day when I finally quiet myself, turn my attention to him, and say, "Speak, for your servant is listening."[1]

As one might expect, each stage is more demanding than the one before it. This is especially true when moving from talking to listening. To be still and allow God to do the talking is a big part of the surrendering that was discussed in Chapter Three, "From Martha to Mary." When I get to this stage, my focus shifts from my own agenda (which I bring to God) to God's agenda (which God brings to me). It also demands a great deal of faith because I am never going to be able to prove to anyone—even to myself— that God is really communicating with me. I will not be able to record God's voice or frame one of his letters to me. I may always have that little voice in my head saying, "Psst! You're making all this up!" I am simply going to have to trust that God is present in my prayer. That is part of the surrendering that prayer demands.

In Chapter Four, "Solitude," I said that the extraordinary moments of solitude, the moments of Being with God, are just that: extraordinary. They are rare and wonderful tastes of the Heavenly Banquet to come. The more typical everyday experience of prayer, then, is at the present level, Listening to God. It is in this third stage that I will spend most of my prayer life. Because it is such a big step, I dedicate the next four chapters to the subject.

A word to the reader. Because the move from stage two to stage three is a really big one, the ideas and concepts presented in the following four chapters are a bit heavier than what you have read so far. If you feel you're getting lost, I suggest three things: (1) Approach someone whom you know has had some experience with contemplative prayer and discuss these topics with him or her; (2) slowly read these chapters several times; and (3) relax! You don't need to understand everything now. File away these insights and retrieve them after you've had a bit of practice praying this way. After some concrete experience, I'm sure you'll be saying to yourself, "Oh, now I get it!"

How Does God Talk Back?

I am frequently asked this question when speaking about prayer: "Once you learn to be quiet and to listen for God's voice, does he actually speak to you? When you ask him something, does he talk back?" The answer is yes; God does talk back, but not in the way that one might expect.

Some Christians mistakenly believe that, in prayer, God removes pray-ers from this earthly sphere and brings them to some higher state of ecstasy completely removed from the dirtiness of the human state. Many people give up on prayer when they do not experience this out-of-body phenomenon. "It doesn't work for me," they'll say. "When I pray, all I feel is my itchy toe or my growling stomach."

The Church has tried to steer itself away from this kind of out-of-body mindset. The reality is that as a human being, I am rooted and grounded in a physical body and mind. I live in a particular reality, a particular place and a particular time, and, because of my finiteness, I cannot leave this reality—not even in prayer.

And why would I want to? *This world* is "charged with the grandeur of God," as Jesuit poet Gerard Manley Hopkins put it. There is no need to leave it. On the contrary, God wants to come to me precisely in the midst of my ordinary day-to-day reality. That is the whole point of the Incarnation—of God becoming human. Therefore, when God talks back, he will do so through the elements of his own creation (even through my itchy toe and growling stomach).

When I share a message I feel I have received in prayer with a skeptical person, he will often say, "Oh, that's just in your head." My response is always, "Of course it is!" My mind is where thoughts are formed and where language is created and received. I cannot converse without it. As a matter of fact, my mind is so much a part of me that I simply do not exist apart from or outside of it. Since it is God who created me this way, why would he not choose to use my mind, my imagination, my emotions to reach me? Would Alexander Graham Bell continue to yell across the street to his neighbor after inventing the telephone?

The biggest hurdle to get over when beginning this stage, then, is to reject this inbred notion that if God speaks at all, it will be only through some extraordinary means—through lightning bolts and levitation experiences. God may come to me in those ways, but like Elijah, most people usually "hear" God's voice in a whisper rather than in an earthquake or a fire.[2]

Praying with Scripture

Scripture is perhaps the most important way that God communicates with Jews and Christians. That is why Christians call the Bible the Word of God. Most contemplative pray-ers consider Scripture their most valuable tool with which to pray and the primary way that God speaks to them in prayer. But before discussing how to listen to God through Scripture, two logistical questions should be considered.

Which translation of the Bible should I use? When *studying* Scripture, it is important to use the most accurate translation of the Bible as possible. That is, the English text should be as literal a translation as possible of the oldest copies of the Scriptures that we have. But when it comes to *praying* over the Scriptures, it is not so important that the translation be precise. The objective in praying over the Scriptures is not to have an intellectual understanding of the text as much as to be moved by it. So I should use whatever translation I'm most comfortable with.

Many Catholics choose to pray with the *New American Bible* because it is the same translation used in the Catholic Mass. Similarly, Protestants may want to pray with the translation normally used at their worship services. The *New Revised Standard Version* is another popular translation for both Protestants and Catholics.

Which passage should I choose to pray over? I can choose either the Gospel passage that is designated for the Mass of the day[3] or some passage that reflects whatever is in my heart or on my mind at the time.[4] Concerning the former, the Church has carefully structured these readings so that if I pray over them every day, I will have read all of the Gospels in three years' time. A third option would be to pray through a Gospel from beginning to end, each day moving a little further along.

I may need to narrow down the passage I choose and read only a small part of it. If, for example, the Sunday reading has three parables included, I may want to pick just one to pray over. Whatever the passage, I should have it open and marked before I begin praying. That way, I don't have to fumble with it during prayer.

How Do You Do It?

I must remember that my objective as a contemplative pray-er is always to lean into being—to come as close to a state of solitude as possible. So, as with other prayer activities, Scripture is used as a means of getting me to greater depths in the ocean of prayer. How, then, do I proceed?

I begin prayer as I described in the chapter on solitude (Chapter Four). If and when I feel ready, I pick up the passage I have prepared and read over it slowly, deliberately and reverently. (Some people find that reading it aloud works better, but I prefer to read it silently. You can experiment to see which way works for you.) As I read it, I am feeling for an opening into solitude. I may read the passage several times while waiting for the quiet to come.

If and when the quiet does come, I lay the Bible down and let myself rest into it. Otherwise, I continue to read the passage again and again, slowly and reverently. Eventually, some small part of the passage (a word, a phrase or a sentence) may resonate with something deep inside me. This is usually a sign that God wants to speak to me through this part. Therefore, I narrow my focus to include only that part, reading the word, phrase or sentence over and over again.

To illustrate what I'm talking about here, imagine a pitch-black room in an enchanted castle at an amusement park. I want to get to the deeper parts of the castle, but I cannot find the door into the next room. I know there must be a secret door somewhere on one of these walls, so I slowly, quietly walk along the walls, knocking and listening, knocking and listening. After a few laps around the room, I sense that one particular spot on one wall has a different sound to it. I stop trying the other walls and knock only on and around that spot. I begin carefully feeling the spot for an opening. Eventually, I find a crevice, which, when pushed will open the door into the next room of the castle.

In my prayer, I read the passage over and over, imagining each phrase to be another spot on the wall. Eventually, one spot in the passage may somehow seem set apart from the rest. One particular word or phrase will touch me on a slightly deeper level than the rest. I sit with that word or phrase for a while, getting a feel for it. Perhaps eventually the spot will not be the word or phrase but an image or emotion that is evoked each time I read it. I roll the word(s), image or emotion over on my spiritual tongue. I swill it as though I were testing the quality of a fine wine. Amidst this process, I will find myself in a different place. Everything else will drop away from my consciousness except for the spot that has brought me here.

Once I am in the quiet, I stay there as long as I feel comfortable. Maybe even the spot is gone now and nothing but God and I are there. I must keep in mind that even Scripture is not an end in itself, but rather is used to find the doors to the place of solitude. Scripture passages are walls on which a door to solitude is hidden.

If I allow them to be ends in themselves, then they will merely be walls, separating me from the next level.

Maybe the word or passage won't slip away. That's OK, too. I will continue to savor that one spot until it becomes a mantra that I chant internally, over and over again. I may stay down in the depths of this ocean the entire prayer time, or it may only last a minute or two. When I do feel myself rising to the surface, I (very gently!) try to descend again, leaning into being. But if, despite my gentle efforts, my spirit continues to rise, then I simply come back to the surface and return to one of my activities. Perhaps I'll feel myself descend again in a few moments; if so, I again drop everything and drift into the peace and quiet. If not, I'll enjoy whatever activity I'm doing.

But How Do You Do It, Really?

Beginners in prayer may find the above description too abstract. (How does one swill a passage, for heaven's sake!?) So, what follows is a sample of what a typical prayer time of mine looks like.

- While sipping my coffee, I flip to the passage I wish to pray over today. For example, I open my Bible to Luke 5:1-11, Peter's Big Catch. I set the open Bible aside, and enjoy the rest of my coffee.

- While sitting there, enjoying the breeze from my open window, I find myself humming the song I heard at Mass yesterday. As I put my empty cup down, I sit in an upright but comfortable position, close my eyes and focus on the song I'm humming, allowing it to bring me into a deeper state of quiet. I stay that way for a short while.

- When it feels right, I pick up the Bible and read over the passage a few times, slowly, reverently and deliberately.

- Each time I read it, I am struck by the phrase, "For he and all who were with him were amazed at the catch of fish that they had taken," so I read that one phrase over and over again, pausing for a while between each reading.

- The image of the overflowing nets becomes more vivid. I put down the Bible, close my eyes and sit with that image, seeing myself in the midst of that scene.

- In my imagination, I see myself as Peter and see Jesus standing beside me. He says to me, "I will fill your nets." I sit with that promise, repeating it slowly and reverently in my mind. "I will fill your nets.... I will fill your nets.... I will fill your nets...."

- Eventually, even this drops away and I sit in the stillness, feeling very close to God—feeling inside God. There is no phrase now—no words at all—and no images. Only God and me.

- Later, I become a little less quiet. I shift a little in my chair. I scratch my itchy elbow. Because I feel myself rising from the bottom, I begin repeating again in my mind, "I will fill your nets."

- After a while, I notice that I continue to rise. I again pick up the Bible and read the passage over, paying particular attention to the parts about the nets and the big catch.

- After a long while, I find myself just sitting there, not in solitude, but nevertheless in a quiet and content state, thanking Jesus for his promise to fill my nets.

- Perhaps after a few minutes I will peek into my cup to see if I could get one last swig of cold coffee before I get up to take a shower.

Note the general pattern of my prayer. I start off on the surface, move a little deeper, then a little deeper, until I reach solitude on the ocean floor. After a while, I feel myself rising. While always leaning into being, I contentedly relax in each level of the ocean. In reality, the pattern is not nearly so well defined and orderly. I may stay in one level ninety percent of the prayer time and never get to a deeper level. I may skip a level, or bob up and down between levels. The reality might be closer to the unpredictable curves of a roller coaster. My objective is not to form some orderly pattern, but to (a) lean into being and (b) enjoy, accept and embrace whatever the Lord brings me.

What follows are a few exercises to use as a springboard for this type of prayer.

Exercise L: The J.O.Y. Meditation

In the J.O.Y. Meditation you meditate on Jesus, Others and Yourself.

1. Before beginning my prayer, I choose some Gospel passage to pray over. I have it open and at my side so that I will not have to fumble with it during prayer.

2. After reaching a state of solitude, I read the passage very slowly, trying to take in everything that is happening in the particular scene. After reading, I try to sink back into the solitude by becoming aware of my breathing again.

3. I focus now on Jesus. What was on his mind and heart that day? How did he feel about the people he was addressing? Why did he say and do these particular things to these particular people that particular day? What was his purpose? What was his message?

4. After a while, I slowly read the Scripture a second time, and then return to my breathing. I reflect on the other characters in the

Gospel story and imagine where they were standing or sitting in relation to Jesus. Why were they there? What were they seeking? What were their thoughts? Their feelings? Their prejudices? Their fears? Their hopes? How do they feel about Jesus at the beginning of the scene? How did these feelings change as the scene progressed?

5. I slowly return to the Scriptures a third time. While breathing slowly, I imagine Jesus now facing me and saying and doing to me what he said and did that day. How am I feeling about Jesus as he speaks and acts? Why is he approaching me in this way? What is he really trying to say to me? How would my life change if I were to allow this gospel message to take root in my heart? How willing am I to make those changes?

6. If I feel called to do so, I say, "Yes!" to Jesus' invitation for transformation within me.

7. I return again to my state of quiet, asking God to transform me into the person the Gospels call me to be.

Exercise M: Where Am I in the Story?

Like the exercise above, this exercise works great with Gospel stories, whether they are parables from Jesus or stories about Jesus.

1. Before beginning prayer, I choose some Gospel passage to pray over. I have it open at my side so that I will not have to fumble with it during prayer.

2. I do one of the solitude exercises from Chapter Four. I ride those quiet waves for a while.

3. I read the passage over several times. I then put the Bible aside and sit in the silence and stillness awhile. If and when I feel ready, I ask God to show me *which of the characters most resembles me today.*

4. I read the passage several times again. In my imagination, I play the role of that character. I try to understand thoroughly that character: her hopes and dreams, her fears and failures. I think about what must have taken place in this person's life before this Bible scene and what changes might have occurred as a result of what happened in the story. I ask God to show me how my own life mirrors that character's life.

5. I draw insights from perceiving myself in light of this character. I talk to God about the insights and ask God to help me to unpack them.

6. I ask God to transform me in and through the insights I have gleaned from my prayer this day.

Note: There are two types of characters I can choose to be that may not immediately come to mind. First, I may choose to play the role of Jesus. This is a great thing to do since I am, in fact, called to be Christ for my own world (see 2 Corinthians 5:16-21). Second, I may also choose to play the role of a character that is not mentioned in the story. I may imagine myself to be the spouse of one of the characters, a bystander in the crowd or even an animal like a camel or a dog.

Exercise N: Where Is the Story in My Life?
This exercise can be used for non-narrative passages, such as those found in the psalms, the prophets (such as Ezekiel or Isaiah) and the epistles (found after the Gospels).

1. Before beginning prayer, I choose the passage I want to pray over. I have it open and ready at my side.

2. I do one of the solitude exercises from Chapter Four. I ride those quiet waves for a while.

3. I read the passage several times. I then put the Bible aside and sit in the silence and stillness. If and when I feel ready, I ask God to show me *what is the central value or vice being spoken of in this passage.* In other words, I ask God to sum up for me the entire passage with just one or two words (for example, hope, gratitude, fidelity, selfishness, idolatry, greed).

4. I read the passage several times again. I ask God to show me the presence of this virtue or vice in my own life right now. I say, "God, please reveal to me the presence of hope (or fidelity or greed) in my life today." I try to experience that virtue or vice—to feel what it's like to have a heart filled with greed, for instance, or to be overwhelmed with a sense of gratitude for all that the Lord has given me.

5. I ask God to show me the consequences of my virtue or vice. In the long run, how does it affect me? How does it affect those with whom I live and work? How does it affect the world?

6. I draw insights from this reflection. I ask God to show me how to live tomorrow based on these insights I've received today—how to foster the virtue of this passage or how to avoid the vice of it.

7. If I feel so inclined, I say "Yes!" to God's invitation to transformation.

Other Ways to Listen to God

Although praying with Scripture is the primary way of listening to God, it is not the only way. The variety of ways of praying in this stage is only limited by my own imagination and enthusiasm. Here are a few examples:

Exercise O: The Chair

1. After reaching stillness, I imagine myself sitting in one of three chairs in an empty room. I begin to reflect on my life at this very moment and ask myself, "Who is the person who is most on my mind right at this moment? My brother? My spouse? My boss? Why is he or she on my mind? What am I feeling deep down in my heart about him or her?" I do not settle on the first answers that I come up with. I keep probing—asking myself these questions until I feel I have reached the core of the issues.

2. I then imagine that very person sitting in one of the empty chairs. I imagine this person telling me everything he or she is feeling about me and about the present situation. I imagine this person speaking without fear, anxiety or embarrassment. What would he or she say? I listen quietly and attentively to the words spoken.

3. I now share with this person what I have discovered are my deep emotions right now. I imagine myself without fear, anxiety or embarrassment and able to say exactly what I am feeling.

4. I now notice Jesus sitting in the third chair listening intently to my conversation. I ask him to tell us his feelings about this situation. What does he say? Is he happy? Disappointed? Does he have some insight the other person and I have not thought of? What is my response? How should my attitude and actions toward this person change because of this encounter with Jesus?

5. If I feel called to do so, I say "Yes!" to Jesus' invitation to transformation.

6. I close by returning to the silence exercises, inviting God to transform my life.

Exercise P: Rerun of the Day

1. After reaching stillness with my silence exercises, I imagine myself in my living room relaxed and quiet after a long day. I notice that the TV is on and that I am watching video clips of my entire day. I note the remote in my hand and begin to fast-forward through the boring parts, trying to find the most interesting moments of the day. When I reach the first one, I put the remote down and watch the scene with my full attention.

2. I focus first on myself. Why was I there? What was I seeking deep down inside? What were my thoughts? My feelings? My prejudices? My fears? My hopes? What did I want or need from the other characters in the scene? How did I feel about them and about myself before this scene? How did my feelings about them and about myself change as a result of what happened?

3. I rewind to the beginning of this scene and watch it again, this time focusing on the others in the scene. Why were they there? What were they seeking? What were their thoughts? Their feelings? Their prejudices? Their fears? Their hopes? What is it that they wanted or needed from me? How did they feel about themselves and about me before this scene? How did their feelings about themselves and me change as a result of this scene?

4. As the scene comes to a close a second time, I notice that Jesus is now sitting beside me on the couch. I imagine him asking me to play back the scene one last time. After doing so, I ask Jesus to comment on it. How does he feel about the situation? About the

other characters? About me? How do I feel about Jesus' response? I dialogue with Jesus about it.

5. Finally, I ask Jesus to tell me where I should go from here. I let him tell me what he would have me do as follow-up to this event. If I feel called to do so, I make a commitment about what I will and will not do tomorrow.

6. I close by returning to the silence exercises, asking God to transform my life.

Exercise Q: Deathbed

This exercise is a way to help me make a big decision about something. It is based on the writings of Saint Ignatius.4 I may want to repeat this exercise several times over the course of my discernment (that is, spiritual decision-making) process.

1. I use one of the solitude exercises from Chapter Four to quiet myself. I allow myself to rest in God's presence for as long as my spirit desires.

2. If and when I am ready, I lay before God the choice I have to make. I spend a while in the Talking to God phase, telling God anything and everything that comes to mind in terms of the various options from which I have to choose.

3. I then imagine that I am actually praying from my deathbed many years into the future. I imagine that I am very close to death and that my whole life is passing before my eyes.

4. I imagine that I am now looking back on the decision that I am presently making. I pretend that I had decided on the first of my choices (let's call it Option A). I imagine myself explaining

to God why I chose Option A. Now here's the crucial question: *How do I feel as I talk to God about the choice that I made? Do I feel ashamed? Proud? At peace? Happy?* Here's the second crucial question: *Why do I feel this way?*

5. I have a conversation with God about the insights I have gleaned from this imagination exercise.

6. I pause a moment and return to the solitude for as long as I can. I then do the deathbed exercise again, now imagining that years ago I chose Option B. I explain to God why I made that choice, reflecting on those same crucial questions, and conversing with God about my reflections.

7. I repeat the exercise using Options C, D, E and so on, until I have reflected on all of my options.

8. After reflecting on all the options, I ask myself the most crucial question of all: *While reflecting on each option, which brought me the most interior peace?*

9. I close by asking God to give me the strength to do what I feel is right. Perhaps I will conclude by praying one of the following ready-made prayers:

Serenity Prayer

God grant me the serenity to accept the things I cannot change, courage to change the things I can, and the wisdom to know the difference.[6]

Saint Ignatius's Prayer for Generosity

Eternal Word, only begotten Son of God, teach me true generosity. Teach me to serve as you deserve—to give without counting the cost, to fight heedless of the wounds, to labor without seeking rest, to sacrifice myself without thought of any reward except for the knowledge that I have done your will.[7]

CONCLUSION

This process of listening to God through the Scriptures and through other means is often referred to as "meditation." It is perhaps the most crucial step in the adventure of learning to pray contemplatively.

NOTES

1. 1 Samuel 3:10.
2. 1 Kings 19:11-13.
3. See USCCB.org for the daily Mass readings.
4. See Appendices for suggestions. You might also want to use another book of mine, *God I Have Issues*
5. *SpirEx*, 186.
6. Friedrich Oetinger.
7. *Hearts on Fire*, Michael Harter, editor (St. Louis, Mo.: Institute of Jesuit Sources, 1993), p. 35.

....

LISTENING TO GOD

- *It is sometimes referred to as:* discernment, meditation, praying with Scripture.

- *Basically it is:* hearing God's voice through Scripture and other means.

- *Some examples include:* placing myself inside a Biblical scene, finding a spot in the passage, imagining a conversation between God and me.

- *The advantages of this type of prayer are:* Together with Talking to God, I now have a personal relationship with God wherein we dialogue with one another; God can show me his perspective on an issue in my life; I can discern God's will for my life.

- *The distortion of this type of prayer is:* perceiving prayer as merely a place where I get answers.

- *The difficulty of this type of prayer is:* distinguishing God's voice and will from my own.

- *The transition to the next level might come when:* I want not just a personal relationship with God, but an intimate one.

chapter eight

READING THE SIGNS OF THE PRAYER TIMES
The Graces of Prayer

The previous chapter explained how God does indeed communicate with me in my prayer, and that he usually does so in the most ordinary ways. God uses my own imagination, intellect and emotions to do so. But how does he do this? What is it like to hear God's voice? How do I recognize that voice? That is the subject of the next two chapters.

DO YOU HEAR WHAT I HEAR?

All along, I have been speaking about *listening* to God, about God *speaking* to the pray-er and about the pray-er *hearing* God's *voice*. This vocabulary of listening, speaking and hearing can be misleading if taken too literally. The notion of hearing God's voice is only an analogy for the way God communicates. As I grow in my prayer life, God begins to communicate with me on a more profound level than that of the five senses. God is not chatty. Yes, he does use words, images and so on, but he chooses each one carefully so that only a few of them are necessary.

If Andreas begins to date someone, the two of them will have to spend a while learning how to communicate with each other. In the beginning, it will take Andreas a long time and a lot of words to get her to understand how he feels about something. As their relationship grows and they get to know each other better, he will be able to communicate those same feelings with much less trouble. After several years, merely a glance at his love will tell her all she needs to know. And by the end of their long life together, she will often know what he's thinking or feeling without even having to look at him.

The same is true for my long and wonderful prayer life with God. In the beginning, I may need a lot of stimuli to help me experience what God is communicating to me. I may need concrete signs to understand God's messages. But after a while, I will be able to *sense* the direction in which God wants to take our relationship. I don't need to actually *hear* God say the words, "I forgive you," for example. I will simply feel that forgiveness deep down.

In Chapter One, I told of a time when I heard God ask me, "Mark, what is it that you desire?" (See "Calling and Commitment," page 1.) There were no magic-show qualities about what happened that night in El Paso: no divine finger, no thunderous clouds, no earthquakes. God's words to me, "What is it that you desire?" were not words in the most literal sense. The experience was more a quiet sense of things. I sensed that was what God was asking of me.

This process of sensing what God has to say to me is a very intuitive one. I must use my gut as much or more than my head to figure it out. An animal trainer who works with a particular animal for a long time can begin to communicate with that animal. They don't learn each other's language (dogs don't speak human and humans don't speak dog), but each can sense what is going on with the other. If I ask that trainer, "What is your dog thinking right now?" the trainer might say, "He's nervous with so many strangers around." Or "He wants you to pet him." If I ask the trainer how she knows this, she probably will have great difficulty explaining it. It's just something she can sense after being with the animal for so long. Likewise, it's very clear that the dog knows when his master is angry, happy, nervous and so on. This mutual sensing of moods is what I'm talking about here.

So I begin to sense certain moods or insights within myself—to recognize a common strand or theme running through a series of prayer times. These themes or moods come in many different forms:

- I may sense God asking me, "What is it you desire?," or telling me, "I will fill your nets."

- Or, I may sense some action God is doing in my soul. I may sense God healing me of some past wound or renewing my fatigued spirit.

- I may sense images too. The face of Jesus laughing or crying may be prevalent in my prayer, or perhaps the image of myself as a lost child could arise.

- The sense may be an attraction to a particular Bible passage. I may feel called to read a particular passage for several days in a row.

- The sense could be some simple but profound insight that keeps popping up in my prayer and in my day. For example, I may be struck by the order of God's creation or the unwavering persistence of God's pursuit of me.

- The sense may be that of a question that is bothering me or a situation that is confusing me. I may be confused or troubled by some teaching of the Church or of the Bible, or I may be bothered by a moral decision that I must make but do not know how.

- A person from my past or present may keep showing up in my prayer. Once while I was on retreat a childhood friend of mine kept coming to mind, so I prayed for her for several days. When I spoke with my mother a week later, she said, "By the way, you should pray for Rebecca because she's going through a rough time now." Imagine the wonder I felt as I told her, "I already have."

- Sometimes the sense is nothing more than an emotion. I may feel deeply sad in my prayer time, or I may have a profound sense of peace, unrest, love or excitement.

- Saint Ignatius said that holy desires, such as the desire to be more active in the Church, or the desire to spend more time with one's family, are especially important.

Spiritual writers use different terms for these common strands that we sense over time. They are called moods, experiences, insights, messages, movements or graces. From this point forward, I will refer to them as graces. Using the term in this way, one could ask, "What has been the grace of your prayer lately?" Or a person returning from a retreat might say to his spouse, "I want to share with you the graces of my retreat." By graces, then, I mean the particular:

    words

    phrases

    experiences

    images

    passages

    insights

    questions

    persons

motions

desires

...that I sense God is planting in the rich soil of my soul.

The Heart of the Matter

Needless to say, not every word, phrase, experience and so on is a grace from God. In fact, most of them that come to me in prayer will be superficial distractions. What I am looking for are the movements that are occurring *deep* within me.

Let me illustrate what I'm talking about here. Let us say that I am taking a cross-country trip with a very close friend of mine, and that on the fourth day of our drive, I become annoyed with him for silly things, such as the way he keeps changing the radio station in the middle of a good song. If someone were to ask me just then, "How do you feel about your friend?" I could answer with my superficial feelings of the day. I could fly off the handle about what's irritating me about him right now. "Honestly, I would just as soon be alone today," I could bark.

But I could answer that same question in another way. I could talk about my deep feelings. I could try to describe how, over the years, my friend and I have been present to each other through very difficult times. I could talk about how we have come to rely on each other for that support and strength. Both ways of answering would be truthful, but the second way really gets at the heart of the matter.

Likewise, when I am praying, a thousand little thoughts and feelings will flutter through my mind and heart like little leaves dancing on the surface of a river. But in prayer, I'm interested in what is happening in the *depths*. If I am praying over a particular Bible passage about Jesus healing a woman, for instance, I can think of all sorts of intellectual insights about it. I can consider the literary form of the passage, the status of women in first-century Palestine, the grammar and syntax of this translation and on and on. But, true though they may be, these thoughts are all superficial. I need to get to the spiritual core of the passage. What is going on below the surface of this Bible story? What is happening in the heart of the woman who has approached Jesus? What is Jesus really trying to accomplish for and with her? The answers to these questions won't be factoids that I could learn from a Bible textbook. They will be more subtle and abstract movements which, like my deep feelings for my friend, are much more difficult to put into words.

'GRACE UPON GRACE'[1]

Many times the response to God's grace that I sense my soul is giving is a grace itself, and one that is as important or more important than God's initial communication to me. By the time I reach this level of prayer, I have surrendered enough to God so that God is now the prime mover in my prayer. God somehow initiates even my responses to him. When God asked me during my desert experience, "Mark, what is it that you desire?" I sensed my soul responding, "I want to be with you, Lord." I did not consider my options and choose this particular response. It welled up within my soul and was as surprising and moving to me as the question.

I said in the previous chapter that God said to me once, "I will fill your nets." Later, in subsequent prayer times, I sensed my soul respond, "I know you will," in the most nonchalant way, as though God were telling me something already obvious to me. I have experienced my nets being filled by God so many times in my life that this statement was no surprise to me. God might as well have said, "The sky is blue." In reviewing my prayer, I realized that my "I know you will" was as important a grace to me as God's "I will fill your nets," because this second grace was the insight that the promise of the first grace had already been fulfilled a thousandfold.

I remember a friend telling me once how much his prayer had been filled with the words from a Tuck and Patti song, "You Take My Breath Away." After having me listen to it, my friend said to me, "The best thing about this song in my prayer is that sometimes I sense God singing it to me; sometimes I sense myself singing it to God and sometimes the song is being sung in my heart with no clear idea of who is singing it to whom."

A Treasure-filled Lake

My first spiritual director, Father Mike Guidry, once gave me a helpful analogy for this phenomenon of receiving graces in prayer:

> I imagine myself in a boat in the middle of a magical lake. At the bottom of the lake are treasures galore. As I sit quietly and gaze into the deep water, I notice that one such treasure is slowly floating to the surface. I wait patiently as the treasure pops up near my boat. I take hold of it and put it in my boat. After admiring it for a long while, I put it down and stare back into the water only to notice another treasure floating to the surface. After taking and admiring this treasure, another starts to float to the top. And another. And another. I spend the whole day watching treasures float up, taking them out of the water, admiring them and putting them into my boat.

The treasures I receive are the graces of my prayer periods. Using this analogy, I note some common characteristics of the process of receiving graces in my prayer.

Sometimes, I have to stare into the water a long time before anything floats up. To say that my prayer life is a matter of one treasure after another floating up is a little misleading. Even on a successful fishing trip with my dad, most of my time will be spent casting my line, not reeling in fish. Likewise, a great deal of my time spent in prayer will involve waiting for the next treasure, feeling for an opening into the solitude, leaning into being. This waiting, feeling and leaning is not wasted time. My soul grows as much or more from waiting on the Lord as from receiving some concrete gift. In fact, the waiting itself is a treasure. Unlike fishing, the casting alone is the catching.

Sometimes, I grow impatient with the slow rate at which the treasure floats up. God's treasures surface in God's own time, which is usually much too slow for my taste. For this reason, I shouldn't put a lot of weight on evaluations of individual prayer times. Instead, I should focus on the overarching movements of several prayer times that surface over a period of weeks or months. One particular day I may find myself in a sour disposition and assume that God is angry when the real source of my problem is that bad liverwurst I had for lunch. If I reflect over longer periods of time, I will be able to weed out food and other external factors.

Sometimes, I grow impatient with the fact that only one treasure at a time floats up. The graces of prayer ultimately lead to a transformation in me. They free me from the bondage of my numerous little sins and deficiencies. Concerning the problem areas of my life, I tend to be much harder on myself than God is on me. I want to fix all my problems immediately and sometimes paralyze myself trying to do so. (Have you heard of the prayer, "I need patience, Lord. And I need it right now"?) God, on the other hand, sees my kennel of barking blunders from an eternal perspective. God will take care of them all in good time. He knows that the problems only escalate when I try to solve them all at once. That is why he seldom sends up more than one treasure at a time.

Sometimes, because it is a magical lake, a treasure will float up without my knowing it until after it has placed itself into my boat. This is an extremely important point. I shouldn't be surprised if I cannot get a clear idea of what grace the Lord has given me until after he has done so. I will often understand what grace I've received only after I've gone through the experience. In Exodus 33:18-23, God tells Moses that he will not be able to see God face to face. If he quiets himself, however, Moses will be able to see "God's back." What this means is that I, as a feeble and finite human, have difficulty seeing God's face. The direct experience of God's presence in my life overwhelms me. I can scarcely take it in. That is why sometimes I can only see God from behind. I only recognize God after he has already passed. I see his footprints in my life and know that he was here. For this reason, the experience I have in my prayer periods sometimes will not make sense until I am looking back on it.

There are even times when I cannot figure out the meaning and purpose of a particular treasure until long after I have stored it away in my boat. Recently, while visiting home, I had the opportunity to read a storybook to my nephews and niece. It was about a fix-it man who never threw anything away. His little shop was filled with pieces of string, chunks of wood, odd-looking screws and so on. When anyone laughed at his pack-rat behavior, he would always smile and say, "There is a use for everything. You never know when you will need a door knob or a pickle jar."

In the end, he saved the day by fixing up a mangled doll for a distraught little girl.[2]

As I grow in my prayer life, my soul becomes a delightfully cluttered attic, filled with random graces that do not all fit together in some perfectly ordered system. The purpose of some graces will be immediately apparent in my life, but the meaning of others might evade me for a while. I must resist the temptation to clean up the messiness of my graces and must not try to come up with immediate answers for the questions that arise from them. This experience of preserving seemingly useless treasures reminds me of the science-fiction video game Myst, wherein the player explores different worlds, picking up objects—a box of matches here, a key there—which will be needed in future worlds.

By way of illustration, let us say that in my prayer periods lately, I have been drawn to the passage about the prodigal son.[3] Upon reflection, I recognize this passage as the grace the Lord is giving me presently. I know that it's from God and that he has a reason for giving me this grace at this time, but I have no idea what that reason is. I don't know what relation this story has to my present life. I ask God, "Why have you brought me to the home of the prodigal son, Lord?" But I get no answer, just a stronger sense that I am to stay in this place for a while.

Sometime later—perhaps even long after I have moved on to other graces—I am faced with a situation wherein an old friend who has betrayed me is now asking for my forgiveness. I am slow to respond because of the pain I still feel from the betrayal. Then, all at once, maybe in my prayer time, maybe in some ordinary moment of my day, I am reminded of the Bible story and am spiritually brought back to the home of the prodigal son. As I watch the familiar scene again, I remember the inner strength it took for the father in the story to open his arms and home to his rebellious son. Moved by such unconditional love and drawing strength from the True Prodigal Father who has done the same for me, I find within myself the grace to surrender my bitterness and welcome my old friend back.

I must accept all the graces that the Lord gives me, even the ones that make little sense to me now. I must store up the spiritual doorknobs and pickle jars because I never know when I will need them.

CONCLUSION

All of the points of this chapter can be summed up by saying that this is God's work in which I am participating. It's all about God's treasures, God's boat and God's lake. So, I am back again to the necessity of surrendering to God—allowing God to be God and myself to be as open and receptive as Mary, who was full of grace.

NOTES

1. John 1:16; see also 2 Corinthians 3:18.
2. Ronnie Peltzman, *Mr. Bell's Fix-it Shop* (New York: Golden Press, Western Publishing, 1981).
3. Luke 15:11-32.

chapter nine

SORTING THROUGH A BIG CATCH (PART ONE)

The Review of Prayer

There is a story of a young Jesuit who said to his superior, "I was just talking with Jesus, and he says that our community should get a new car." The superior looked up at him and said, "That's funny, I was just talking to Jesus's father, and he says we ought to make do with what we've got."

I may be saying to myself at this point, "OK, I believe that God can speak to me through my imagination, intellect and so on. I know that I will be able to sense what it is that God is communicating to me. But isn't it true that it could just be me talking to myself? Might I not be simply putting in the mouth of God the words that I want to hear?" Unfortunately, the answer is yes. I can indeed deceive myself into believing that other voices are the voice of God. For this reason, it is nec-essary to review prayer—to look back on my recent prayer times and sort through what is really from God and what is not.

But there is a second reason for the review of prayer. The word *grace* refers to an unmerited gift of God. It is the manifestation of God's generosity. When I use this word to refer to the movements that occur in one's prayer time, the implication is that these graces we experience in prayer are precious gifts and tokens of God's love. They are neither assignments (though I may be spurred to do something), nor rebukes (though they may remind me of my unworthiness), nor rewards (though they may reveal to me my strengths), nor purchased commodities (though they are of tremendous value to me). They are gifts, and gifts are to be cele-brated. That is ultimately what I am called to do with this grace I have received. I must rejoice in it. Relish it. Savor it. Prayer is not a business negotiation whereby I agree on a price, pay it, receive my goods and then leave. Prayer is a banquet at which there are no time limits, only slow savory courses.

So, the reasons I review my prayer are (a) to sort out what is the treasure and what is not and (b) to relish, give praise for, and deepen the experience of the particular grace I am pres-ently receiving. After a few preliminary remarks, this chapter will discuss these two reasons for the review of prayer. The next chapter will describe five concrete ways of doing so.

PRELIMINARY REMARKS

Prayer is for listening; review of prayer is for discerning. It is important that I resist the temptation to analyze my prayer time while it is going on. During prayer, I will be tempted to play the sports commentator, reviewing every move with instant replay. I will be tempted to ask myself if the prayer is going well, if it is really God speaking or merely my imagination, if I'm handling this conversation well and so on. This ongoing analysis will only distract me from listening for God with my full attention. It is rather like the nervous boy on a date who spoils the fun of it by constantly asking his date, "Are you enjoying yourself?" He may be so concerned with how the process is going that he doesn't pay attention to the girl at all. In the same way, I may miss God's voice because I am too preoccupied with evaluating the prayer then and there. During the prayer itself, I must simply be present and listen attentively to whatever is said by whomever. There will be plenty of time to sort it all out later.

When I pray, I spend quality time with God, not quantity time. Prayer is not a drive-through-fast-food-style answering service. When I set about the task of praying, my motivation should be to enter into an intimate relationship with God, not to get divine fortune cookies about where my life will go. Therefore, when I evaluate prayer, I should not do so on the basis of how much I get out of it. As will be discussed later, *what* comes out of my prayer time is not nearly as important as *who* comes out of my prayer time. The most intimate moments I've had with God have been after we've gone through our "business"—what I wanted to say to God and what he wanted to say to me—and simply sat quietly together like the porch-sitting Savoys.

In the midst of the important things God says to me, I will have a thousand silly daydreaming sorts of thoughts. This is completely normal. Chapter Eleven, "When Things Go Haywire," discusses how to deal with distractions. For now, suffice it to say that they're no big deal. I should take the advice of Richard Carlson's book title, *Don't Sweat the Small Stuff.*

Finally and most important, there is no such thing as a bad prayer period. My prayer time may be boring, distracted, frustrating, upsetting, confusing and so on, but if it was true prayer, then God will make good use of it. I will never understand fully what God is thinking in that omniscient brain of his. God may actually be the cause of my prayer's boredom or distraction because it is the only way for me to learn the particular lesson he is presently trying to teach me. So, a frustrating prayer period that I am so quick to call "bad" may actually have gone precisely as God intended it.

The First Reason for Reviewing Prayer:
Fool's Gold and Hidden Treasures

"The kingdom of heaven is like a net that was thrown into the sea and caught fish of every kind; when it was

full, they drew it ashore, sat down, and put the good into baskets but threw out the bad..."—Matthew 13:47-48

The spoils of a great sea-treasure hunt do not go directly from the ocean floor to some museum case. They must first be sorted through, cleaned and examined. The stones must be thrown away, the mud and muck must be washed off and the barnacles must be carefully removed. Likewise, a grace in prayer will come to me in the midst of crazy thoughts, itchy toes and all kinds of other irritating distractions. Once I have identified the grace, I must spend some time with it, "cleaning" it—separating it from the useless stuff.

Among the items of my big catch, I may find some fool's gold—useless rocks that are so beautiful they seem to be treasures at first. For example, some of my own petty desires may be dressed up to look like treasures from God. These desires sometimes disguise themselves into the appearance of a grace from God. I may be madly in love with a person who is no good for me. My lovesickness may convince me that the grace I am receiving in prayer is a calling to marry the person when nothing could be farther from the truth.

Other parts that need to be removed are the well-intentioned but ill-advised acts of a zealous pray-er. Beginners in prayer are especially prone to inspirations to go out and do something extraordinary for God. Needless to say, if these inspirations are from God, which is often the case, then it is a wonderful beginning of a new life in Christ. But from time to time, my unbridled enthusiasm has me doing things that on the surface seem like great acts, but in the end, are misguided.

Father Gene Tremie, a priest from my childhood years, once told a parable about what I am here calling fool's gold:

There was once a small country town that had only one little chapel where all went to pray every Sunday. One day the devil, dressed in the form of a wealthy philanthropist, came to town and donated a beautiful bell for the heretofore-barren steeple. Now why did he do that?

It seems the poor townspeople owned no watches or clocks and since there was no church bell, they all gathered early in the morning and waited around for Mass to start. While waiting, the men and women sat under the trees, visiting with one another while their children played in the churchyard. By the time Mass began, the people knew who had died, what new babies were born, whose tractor had broken down and so on. They took all of this with them as they began to pray together at Mass. Later that week, it was not unusual for the farmer with the broken tractor to have visiting neighbors driving onto his fields atop their own tractors, raring to get to work. And in the homes of young mothers with newborns, there suddenly appeared older mothers sweeping, cooking and cleaning.

After installing the spiffy new church bell, however, the people didn't get to the churchyard until the bell tolled—no more visiting before and no more lending a hand afterwards. Even the Mass seemed empty, since the believers had only their own joys and sorrows to bring to the altar.

Like the new church bell, some of the seemingly beautiful and holy acts that beginners in prayer are spurred on to do are actually detrimental and could even stunt their spiritual growth. The once dedicated father is now too busy volunteering at church to play with his kids. The once hard-working mother now sits all day in the shade of her tree, praying the rosary. The solitary pilgrimage to the Holy Land replaces the annual family vacation. The homeless lie in the streets, shivering in the cold, while the Church volunteer corps builds an additional chapel in the churchyard.

For this reason, I must submit the grace I have received to the tests of time and scrutiny. Jesus says, "You will know them by their fruits" (Matthew 7:16-17), so I must let the grace germinate a while and then observe (that is, review) what fruits come of it. Only after a thorough review of prayer will I have a better idea of the source of the experience. The various methods of review (which will be presented in the next chapter) comprise a sort of checks-and-balances system to weed out some of the misinterpretations of my graces.

My review of prayer, then, may reveal some fool's gold, which needs to be thrown out. But the good news is that the review may also uncover a few hidden treasures, as well. There may be seemingly useless experiences, insights or emotions in my prayer that I am inclined to discount as mere distractions, but which turn out to be diamonds in the rough.

Even painful experiences in prayer, such as resurrected memories from some difficult part of my past, may actually turn out to be experiences of accepting, forgiving, embracing and healing. There also will be times in my prayer life when the Lord will need to cauterize some diseased parts of my spirit. There is a wonderful image in the Old Testament book of Jeremiah in which the Lord is a sculptor and his people are his clay creation (see Jeremiah 18:1-6). The Lord shows Jeremiah that he must break the old mold to recreate his people into something new. This breaking is as painful as it sounds. Part of my commitment to prayer is to allow the Lord to purify my spirit. So when I speak of "treasures" in my prayer, I do so from a faith perspective that does not allow for bad gifts from God. I must believe that every one of God's oysters has a hidden pearl inside. I need the prayer review to crack open that oyster.

THE SECOND REASON FOR REVIEWING PRAYER: SAVORING EVERY BITE

I also return to the grace of the prayer to relish and rejoice in it. Like the tenth leper who returned to Jesus in praise and thanksgiving (see Luke 17:11-19), I return to the spot where I met Jesus and give thanks and praise for that encounter. Like the disciples running home to tell their friends what had happened to them on the road to Emmaus, pray-ers review the graces of their prayer times, asking in wonder, "Were not our hearts burning within us while he was talking to us on the road?" (Luke 24:13-35).

Just as the Sacrament of Matrimony makes more real the love that the couple already share with each other, so too, when I return to the altar of God to celebrate the wonders he has done for me, I experience those graces in a deeper, richer way.

In this very act of thanksgiving for graces received, I am often bowled over by the richness of the graces I have received. This process of reviewing my prayer in thanksgiving will lead to whole new perspectives on God's gifts to me, so that the original grace becomes a seed, sprouting more and more graces until they are bursting at the seams of my soul. A very common characteristic of the saints is that as they grow in their relationship with God, their sense of gratitude grows until their lives are brimming over with thankfulness, smitten with the realization of the blessings and love of God in their lives. They sing out with the psalmist,

You prepare a table before me
in the presence of my enemies;

you anoint my head with oil;
    my cup overflows. (Psalm 23)

Conclusion

So I must review my prayer for two reasons. First, I do so as a way of receiving clarity. By reviewing my prayer, I begin to sort out the graces from the garbage. Second, I review my prayer as a means of relishing, savoring, deepening and rejoicing in the grace, praising God for the wonders he has done for me. The following chapter discusses several concrete ways of reviewing prayer.

chapter ten

Sorting through a Big Catch (Part Two)
Five Ways to Review Prayer

In the previous chapter, I discuss the reasons why I must review my prayer on a regular basis. In this chapter, five concrete ways of doing so are presented.

The First Way: Placing the Grace on the Altar

Saint Ignatius says that after receiving an important grace from God and acknowledging it as such through reflection, I should bring it back to prayer. In the depths of my prayer, I should place it on the altar of God as an offering—as a way of saying to God, "This is what I feel you have given me, Lord. Now I offer it back to you."

Saint Ignatius says that I am to bring a grace back to prayer in order to receive confirmation from God that this is indeed the treasure I am to hold and to cherish. He says that after making an important choice about how to integrate the grace into one's life, the pray-er "must [re]turn with great diligence to prayer...and offer God his choice that He may deign to accept and confirm it if it is for His greater service and praise."[1]

How does this work? Let's say that I am a young college student who has been praying contemplatively for about a year. Several months ago, I had a strong sense that God is calling me to give my life to him in some special way. I don't know what this means or even if it really comes from God or from my own enthusiasm, so

I take it back to prayer. I pray over Scripture passages that apply to this theme. I converse with God about what this grace might mean and so forth. In doing so, I get an even stronger sense that this is a true calling. Later, as I continue to pray over it, I begin to sense that this calling is to join the Jesuits. My image of Jesuits living, working and praying in their own particular way excites my spirit in an inexplicable way. I again seek confirmation of this grace. I keep bringing the subject up with God in prayer, asking for some sense of his, "Yes, that's it!" After a long while and a lot of prayer, I still feel this tremendous desire in prayer to join the Jesuits. So I apply, am accepted and become a Jesuit novice.

But even novitiate is a time of discernment. During this two-year period, I continue bringing my now concrete experiences of Jesuit living to prayer, asking God for confirmation that this indeed is the life for me. At this point, I may again get a sense of God saying, "Yes, that's it!" or I may get a different sense. I may sense that God does not want me to spend my life here. Perhaps I will begin to sense that God is calling me elsewhere. If this is the new grace that I sense, then I take that back to prayer, asking God to confirm this new calling to leave the novitiate. Maybe God will confirm it, or maybe God will show me that this desire to leave is just awkwardness in my new life as a Jesuit.

So the pattern of my prayer becomes a cycle of receiving some grace in prayer, taking that grace back to prayer for confirmation, feeling affirmed in this grace (or not), receiving some new grace to go beyond the last one, asking for confirmation of this new grace and so on.

Needless to say, less life-changing graces do not need so much time of prayerful consideration. To the extent that I feel called to make important changes in my life because of the grace—to that extent I should test that grace in order to ensure that it is specifically what God is calling me to. The authenticity of most graces, in fact, is self-evident and does not require so much discernment. If the grace I am presently receiving is a simple sense of being enveloped in God's love, for example, I can feel pretty confident that this is from God! How I am to live as one loved by God may be God's next step with me. And this will require quite a bit of discernment.

I also bring the grace back to prayer as a way of deepening the experience of it. Graces from God have no definable entry or exit. They often slip into my life without my noticing it and they stay with me for an indiscernible period. Because society has taught me to be fast and efficient, I can sometimes cut off the grace before it has ripened. I may mistakenly think that the richness I have already experienced from this grace is all there is. Meanwhile, I have only seen the tip of the iceberg. "What no eye has seen, nor ear heard, / nor the human heart conceived,/what God has prepared for those who love him" (1 Corinthians 2:9). God is only beginning to pour forth his blessing through this particular treasure. Saint Ignatius encourages repetitions of important movements for this very reason. When I receive an important grace, I go back to it again and again and again, squeezing all the juice out of it until I have savored every bit.

THE SECOND WAY: JOURNALING

Dear Lord,

You woke me up early this morning and I think it was just because you wanted me to see the sunrise and because you were lonesome for me. I feel your presence so strongly this morning, Lord. I am overwhelmed by it. It's so strong that I feel like I'm going to burst. I am a broken vessel,

Lord, but can you use me anyway? Can you make me strong enough to hold even you inside me? *(Excerpt from a recent prayer-journal entry)*

Reflecting on my graces through journaling can be an enriching experience. A prayer-journal is a spiritual scrapbook of the graces God has sent me throughout my prayer life. The journal can help clarify exactly which grace I am presently receiving. Just as a scientist may not understand what she is observing until she walks away from her experiment, and, with pencil and paper, works out the math, so I too must often work out the problems of my prayer experiences.

There are various ways of journaling. I can write every day or only every now and then. I can address the entries to God, myself, or to whomever is on my mind at any given time. I can write pages and pages or just a few lines. I can make it strictly confidential or I can share it with others. It might contain only my own written entries or it might be filled with poems, cutouts from magazines, a Christmas card that touched me, famous quotes I really like, songs, artwork, dreams, letters and so on. There is no right or wrong way to journal. I can custom fit it to match my own particular personality.

The experience of journaling is often a prayer itself. There have been times when I have been as much or more spiritually and emotionally affected through the journaling time than through the prayer time. It is as though the grace was seeking some way of articulating itself and could not be fully realized until it found such a medium.

One of the advantages of reflecting on a journal is that I can place the grace I am presently receiving in context with the graces I have already received in the past. I can go through my journal asking myself, "How is this grace related to similar graces I have received throughout my prayer life?" Exploring such a question would help me to clarify what I am experiencing now. When I take my present grace and look back through my journal, I am often struck by the realization that God has always loved me in this way.

At times, a present grace will fit together with some grace or graces of the past to reveal a whole picture that I had not comprehended before. (Remember the fix-it man?) This whole picture is not a reheated leftover, but a brand-spanking-new grace from God. That is why the experience of journaling can be such a prayerful one.

I know a family whose kids have a birthday ritual of standing with their backs against their bedroom doorframe while Dad makes a pencil mark to note the child's height. Beside the mark, the date is written. Over the years, the doorframe becomes a visible sign of their growth. Because the journey of prayer is a slow and mysterious one, it is not always easy to see patterns of growth in my relationship with God. This, again, is where a journal can help. Looking back over the years of journal entries, my own growth is vividly apparent to me.

THE THIRD WAY: SHARING THE GRACE WITH A FRIEND

I know few, if any, people who have been able to remain faithful to their prayer lives without the support of a friend or two who share the same desires and convictions. Unfortunately, many have trouble finding such friends. It takes a special person to be able to share with her or him the most intimate movements within one's soul. But God has created me as a part of a people and as such I am driven to share myself with others.

A spiritual friend can join me in celebration of and thanksgiving for the graces of my prayer. The treasures I receive in prayer are too wonderful for me to keep to myself. I've got to share them with others. I need others to rejoice with me over the wonders the Lord has worked in my life. Like Mary visiting her cousin Elizabeth, I need a companion to whom I can joyfully exclaim,

"My soul magnifies the Lord,

and my spirit rejoices in God my Savior,

for he has looked with favor on the lowliness of his servant."

(Luke 1:46-48)

This faith sharing will also serve as a reality check. I need my friends—who are standing outside the experience and, therefore, can have greater objectivity—to tell me whether this experience I am having is a true one. When I fall in love, for example, my objectivity goes out the window (that's why it's called "falling"). I need my friends at this time more than ever because they will be able to tell me whether I'm falling in the right direction—whether I am in love with a real person or with an illusion I have created in my mind. A life of prayer is an experience of falling in love with God. But I need my friends to tell me when it is the true God I am loving and when it is merely a god I have created in my mind to suit my own needs and wants.

A friend could help me to further discern or deepen the experience. He or she could help me to reflect on what this grace might mean for my life—how my life might change because of it. The friend might also have similar experiences to share with me that can give me a new perspective on the experience.

The experience of sharing one another's graces is enriching for both parties. My friends and I nourish and are nourished by the stories that we share with one another. I remember my friend Ray describing a spiritual insight that his friend, Maria, had received in prayer. Ray explained to me how this insight had consequently fed his own prayer life. After this conversation with Ray, the same treasure floated up in my prayer, too. Imagine that: a third-hand treasure, and as good as new!

THE FOURTH WAY: SHARING THE GRACE WITH A SPIRITUAL MENTOR

A teenager once told me how he had dealt with his father's absence in his life. "I've had to go out and find my own father figures," he said. I have found this to be a profound insight that can also apply to the spiritual life. It is important to have at least one or two spiritual mothers and fathers who will see that I "grow up" into a mature pray-er. The spiritual friend mentioned in the third way above cannot take the place of a spiritual mentor. A friend is someone who is more or less on the same level as I am. A mentor or guide is one who has gone ahead of me. The mentor has already gotten through the sometimes tricky first steps and now has the ability to guide others through them.

Finding a spiritual mentor can be even more difficult than finding a spiritual friend. This particular path of contemplation is a unique one. I cannot assume that just because a person is a member of the clergy or a prayerful layperson, she or he will be an experienced contemplative pray-er. Even if I do find an experienced pray-er, there is no guarantee that I will be able to relate well with that person. Perhaps I will discover that this person is not as deep a pray-er as I thought. Maybe I will find his or her communication skills lacking. Maybe I can't even put my finger on why I'm not comfortable with this person; I simply know that it isn't working. Whatever the reason, a person cannot be my mentor unless I am comfortable sharing with and listening to her or him. It is better to have no mentor at all than one with whom I am uncomfortable.

What is the role of a mentor? There are three ways I have been helped by my spiritual mentors. The most important way is through the listening that they do. Having to articulate to another what treasures are floating to the top of my prayer deepens the experience for me. Countless times I have walked away from such conversations saying to myself, "Wow, I can't believe I said that!" Often, it is only through this process of having to explain myself to another person that my prayer life begins to make sense to me.

The second way is through the questions and comments that they make. A good mentor will not judge my prayer or try to control it. He or she will simply make observations about it and ask questions that will stimulate further reflection within me. They often say things like, "Have you ever thought about...?" or "Maybe it's just that...." Mentors help me recognize whatever lenses I'm presently using to read the signs of my prayer times, and they challenge me to consider using new lenses.

Finally, mentors can be a great help through the encouragement they give. When I am sad, angry or confused, my perception of what is going on is often askew. My mentor will calm me down and help me to put things back into proper perspective.

Over the past thirty years or so, the profession of spiritual director has blossomed in the Catholic Church. A spiritual director is someone who is professionally trained to guide others in their prayer lives. Ideally, every beginner in prayer should see a spiritual director regularly. Anyone interested in doing so, but not knowing how to get started, might call the spiritual life office of the local diocese and ask if there are professional spiritual directors in the area. Another place to start might be through calling a local retreat house and asking if they provide ongoing spiritual direction, and if they don't, ask if they can suggest a place that does.[2]

At the risk of being redundant, I must caution that having professional training in spiritual direction does not make this person the right one for me. I should be as picky about whom I choose as my director as I am about my choice of doctors, therapists and dentists. If I sense that the director does not really understand me, that he or she talks too much or too little, that the advice given does not resonate with my experience, or that for some unknown reason, we simply do not fit, I should not hesitate to let the director know this, and if the problem persists, change directors.

THE FIFTH WAY: SHARING THE GRACE WITH MY FAITH COMMUNITY

Not only do I need friends who share in my desires and convictions, and not only do I need mentors who can support, encourage and advise me as I journey to God, but I also need a community with whom I can participate in the proclamation of the Word and the celebration of all that the Word means to me. Like the baby Jesus, I need a "holy family" to belong to. I need to belong to something bigger than myself. If I don't, then I run the risk of developing a sort of God-and-me spirituality with no support systems to hold me up when I am weak, no prophets to challenge me when I am wrong and no party-mates with whom I may celebrate the Lord's goodness in my life.

If possible, it is also good to belong to faith communities within faith communities. This is especially true if my local church is a large one. As part of my experience of Church, I might belong to a Bible study group, a community service organization, a choir, a prayer group and so on. All of these circles within the big circle will serve to make me a vital part of the Church rather than simply an anonymous worshiper in the back pew.

As a pray-er, I bring my graces with me when I go to church. I place these graces in the context of the Word that I hear and of the worship in which I participate. As in the case of my friends and my mentors, my faith community can help me to celebrate the graces that are true, to weed out the ones that are not and to prepare for more of both in the future.

Conclusion

So then, I can review the graces of my prayer through seeking further confirmation in prayer, through journaling, through sharing with a friend and a spiritual director and through celebrating those graces with my faith community or local church. These five ways of reviewing prayer, taken together, serve as a support system, a reality check and a means of celebration and thanksgiving. Without them, my prayer life will be greatly lacking. With them, there is no limit to what the Lord can do for me, personally, and for his people whom I am called to serve through the graces given to me in prayer.

Notes

1. *SpirEx*, 183.
2. See Appendix B for more suggestions.

chapter eleven

WHEN THINGS GO HAYWIRE
Dealing with Distractions

In the next three chapters, I discuss two apparent problem areas in prayer. This chapter discusses the problem of superficial distractions that keep me from being focused in prayer. The two that follow this one discuss the more important issue of dryness in prayer.

ON THE NEW ORLEANS SAINTS, SNAKES AND OTHER DISTRACTIONS

Here's a not-so-unusual sample of what might be going on inside :

Come, Lord Jesus...Come, Lord Jesus...Come, Lord Jesus...*<burp>* Oh, that barbecue just isn't sitting right in my stomach...still, it was nice of Fred to grill some burgers tonight—Pray, Mark! Pray!... Come, Lord Jesus... Come, Lord Jesus...Fred has really been a great friend to me. I hope he wasn't offended when I teased him about his cooking. That was a really stupid thing to say. I can't believe I said that—Come on, Mark, Pray! Sorry, Lord. Come, Lord Jesus...Come, Lord Jesus...Come, Lord Jesus...Shoot! I forgot that the Saints are playing against the right now! Come, Lord Jesus...I hope somebody's recording it. ...Come, Lord Jesus...Come, Lord Jesus...I can't believe I'm thinking about football during prayer; what the heck is my problem here? Come, Lord Jesus...I

guess I'm just distracted. Come, Lord Jesus...as distracted
as Drew Brees was last week...Come, Lord Jesus....

I could go on, but I think you get the point.

As a beginner in prayer, I might find myself complaining: "My
prayer is full of distractions. I try to speak and listen to God,
but then my foot starts itching, or my mind starts wandering off
on some tangent or a thousand crazy images fly by in my head,
and before I know it, I have completely lost my state of quiet."
These distractions might be so nagging that they discourage me
and make me feel that I have failed at the task of prayer. I might
run to books and spiritual guides desperately seeking a solution—
wanting to learn the tricks that would rid my prayer of these crazy
thoughts and that would allow me to reach a state of utter silence.

No one is impervious to distractions. One of the most important
mystics of our day, Trappist monk Thomas Merton said, "If you
have never had any distractions, you don't know how to pray."[1]
These random thoughts are normal and natural phenomena of my
mind, and while they can be diminished, they can never be fully
expelled. I am created with this wondrous contraption called the
brain, which, praise God, cannot be turned off at will.

While there are a few tricks that will help me to focus better,
they are not the most important things to learn about distractions. This is what is important to know: *My anxiety, distress,
guilt and anger about the distractions are far more detrimental
to my prayer than the distractions themselves.* The most effective
way to diminish the distractions, then, is not to worry about them
at all—I don't give them a second thought (literally). That second
thought is yet another distraction and, therefore, a trap into an
endless loop of (a) the initial distraction— "the game" is playing
now"—and (b) worry over the initial distraction—"I can't believe

I'm thinking about football during prayer." While there is only a little I can do to rid myself of the initial distractions, there is much I can do to free myself from anxiety about them. This is what actually distinguishes a mystic from a novice pray-er. Mystics often have as many distractions as novices do, but the difference is in their perception of and their reaction to them.

Perhaps a fable will help to clarify this point.

When I was a child, my dad used to take me fishing in the swamps of Louisiana. Imagine with me for a moment that early one morning on one of these trips, my mind has wondered to far-off lands and heroic adventures. Returning to reality after one of these reveries, I am alarmed to discover a snake coiled around a branch directly above us. I leap to my feet and begin jumping up and down, screaming, "Daddy, Daddy, Daddy!" and pointing to the sinister-looking serpent. Dad, having to withdraw from an exciting struggle with a large catfish at the end of his line, tries to calm me by saying, "It's OK, Mark. It won't hurt you. Take it easy." I, of course, hear none of this over my shrieks and wails. It isn't long before I flip over backwards into the water hitting the old dead branch above with my fishing pole and sending it (along with the snake, its innocent occupant) crashing down onto the aluminum floor of the boat. In a matter of moments (an eternity to me), my dad manages to toss the baffled and distraught snake far away, and to pull me back into the boat, sopping wet and battle-weary. Dad, being the saint he is, comforts me all the way back to the landing. He never speaks a word of his disappointment over the empty ice chest or over the two lost fishing poles, one from my fall and the other from Dad's mighty catfish swimming away with rod and reel in tow.

In this story, which of the two was more of a problem, the snake or my panic over the snake? A no-brainer, right? Of course, the problem was with my *perception* and *response* to the snake. Now, as two adult fishermen, Dad and I enjoy observing (quietly and from a distance) snakes, alligators, hornets' nests and the like. We may be fishing one day when a water moccasin swims by the boat. "Hey, Dad, look who's come to say, 'Hello'," I'll say and the two of us watch as the snake swims past and on to other interests. It has absolutely no impact on our fishing. The situation of distractions is no different. The initial distraction poses little or no threat to my prayer unless I perceive it to be a threat. The way to deal with these little thoughts, then, is simply to watch them pass by.

The same is true, by the way, for physical distractions such as an itchy nose that no scratching seems to satisfy. This is sometimes a chronic problem for beginners. It is probably more an indication of psychological nervousness than a physical problem. If I get an itch, I scratch it. If it comes back, I ignore it. If it persists, Anthony De Mello suggests that I then reverse my strategy and, without moving, focus every part of my consciousness on that one tiny spot on my body. I make it a prayer by thanking God for creating those little cells that are presently itching. Like the water moccasin, the itch will usually just disappear and I can go on with my prayer.

What about the times when there are lots and lots of mental critters running, swimming, flying by my prayer so that it is almost impossible to concentrate? Here's where a few little techniques will help. But before turning to these, I must remember that *prayer is not an assignment from God wherein I must accomplish some task*. I trust in God and relax because whether I catch any fish or simply watch the passing critters, I will do it in God's presence, and no time with God is wasted time.

A FEW TRICKS

- I don't fight distractions; I negotiate with them by acknowledging their presence and then letting them leave on their own. Jesuit Father Thomas Green suggests thinking of them as small children interrupting my visit with a friend.[2] Instead of arguing or scolding, I simply look at them and kindly say, "The adults are talking now, so please go and play in your room." I can also speak directly to God about the distraction. I can say, "God, I'm distracted by football tonight." Simply making this acknowledgment will often release the distraction's hold on me.

- What if they still persist? I try using a mantra in my prayer (see Exercise B of Chapter Four). The mantra will serve as an anchor for my boat, keeping the boat steady so that I don't drown in the waters of distraction. In the sample "football prayer" at the beginning of this chapter, the repetition of "Come, Lord Jesus," is an example of a mantra. By coordinating it with my breath, the breathing itself naturally returns me to the mantra. Waves of distracting thoughts come by and throw me off course a little, but hanging on to this mantra-anchor keeps me from straying too far.

- What if they *still* persist? I vary my prayer activities. I go back to reading the Bible or praying the rosary, the Office and other ready-made types of prayer. Like the mantra, they will give my restless mind something to focus on. But I must be careful. Anthony De Mello tells a story of a young man who, after many years of wooing, finally had his dream girl beside him one day.

Unfortunately, he spent the entire afternoon reading to her the unsent love letters he had written to her all those years and never really enjoyed her presence. The point is that I may spend so much time reading prayers *about* God that these prayers and readings ultimately become distractions themselves, and will keep me from actually encountering God. So I allow these activities to re-center me when I'm feeling unfocused, but I take care not to become obsessed with them. Otherwise, I would merely be replacing one distraction with another.

What if they yet *still* persist? Sometimes the only way out of a problem is by going straight through it. If the distractions do not go away, then I offer my crazy prayer up to the Lord and let him worry about it. I say to God,

> "Lord, it seems as though all I can do today is call out your name in a fog of distractions. Please be present in the fog, Lord, turning its droplets into holy water." I laugh at my stupid thoughts. I accept the messiness. I embrace the madness. I imagine God and me sitting on the Savoys' porch doing nothing more than watching the distractions go by. There is a poignant story of a saintly Zen master who said of his prayer near the end of his life, "...and as for distractions, let them come. I rather enjoy them."

Working through Them

The four exercises in this chapter are samples of the ways I can handle distractions. All of them begin with the presumption that I am in the middle of my prayer time and—despite my gentle efforts—some particular distraction(s) will not go away. These first two exercises assume that my prayer is filled with silly frivolous little distractions.

Exercise R: Offering Up Pesky Distractions

1. Once I have decided that these distractions simply won't go away, I change strategies and now focus on them. I imagine myself quietly, reverently placing each distraction on the altar of my soul. Even if many of the distractions are silly and meaningless, I offer them all up to the Lord.

2. I smile and say to God, "Well, Lord, this is the best I can do today. Please accept these meager gifts."

3. All the while that I am placing these distractions on the altar, I use the mantra *Totus tuus* ("totally yours"), telling God that all in my life—even these silly little thoughts—are his.

Exercise S: The Savoys' Porch

1. Once I have decided that my distractions simply won't go away, I change strategies and now focus on them. I imagine myself sitting on the Savoys' porch sipping coffee and enjoying the rest.

2. I imagine all of these distractions as little critters that run by on the road in front of the house.

3. I invite Jesus to sit with me on that porch and enjoy the show. The two of us calmly, quietly watch the distractions go by, commenting on what we see, but not taking any of the distractions (or even ourselves!) very seriously this day.

WHEN THE SNAKE JUMPS INTO THE BOAT

What we have been dealing with here are what I call trivial distractions. But sometimes the most persistent of these turn out to be worthy distractions. That is, they are not really distractions at all but the very treasure (grace) that God wants to offer me that day.

As a high school theology teacher, I often had my students pray in silence a few minutes and then tell me what happened in their prayer. One day, a sophomore said to me, "I didn't pray at all because I couldn't stop thinking about the big math test I'm taking this afternoon. I tried to stop thinking about it and to get back to God, but the harder I tried, the more it bothered me."

Two points can be made about this: First, this boy's fifteen-minute struggle to grow closer to God *was* prayer, a beautiful and self-sacrificial one at that. Second, maybe it was God who kept bringing up the math test in his prayer! The boy could have then *used* the distraction as the focal point of his prayer. He could have imagined himself simply placing that test on the altar of God and saying, "God, please bless my struggles with math and with any other hard tasks I have to face today."

The boy also could have deepened the prayer by allowing the thought to become a springboard for further reflection. Maybe he was obsessed with studying and should have surrendered his anxiety to God's providential care. Or maybe he could have asked God's forgiveness for his lack of studiousness. The boy could have spent the time thanking God for the rare gift of a good education. Or perhaps the whole notion of math could have left him awestruck at God's order in the universe. These types of reflections are ways of *consecrating* the distraction. What better prayer could one ask for? Again, what hindered the boy was not the thought of the math test, but his perception that the thought would keep him from God.

To use a different example, I may have trouble quieting my spirit because I am worried about a sick friend in the hospital. If it is a healthy concern, then it is an act of love and is, therefore, a worthy distraction. So as I sit beside her hospital bed while she sleeps, I might spend a prayer time imagining my friend breathing in the healing Holy Spirit. I may spend the prayer thanking God for the gift of my friendship with this person. Or I may recite prayers of petition, asking God to give courage to my friend, wisdom to the doctors, stamina to her family and so on.

Exercise T: *Worthy People Distractions*

This exercise begins with the presumption that I am in the middle of my prayer time and am having trouble quieting myself because of some worthy distraction about a person in my life.

1. Once I have decided that this distraction is worth praying over, I change strategies and now focus on it. If the distraction involves some other person (that I am worried about, angry with, in love with, etc.), I focus all of my attention on that person. I ask God to show me that person through his eyes. I continue reflecting on God's perception of this person as long as I am able.

2. I ask God to show me his perception of my relationship with this person. For example, if I'm in love, I ask for God's impression of the relationship: "Is it true love, God? Is it healthy love? Am I handling the relationship in accordance with the gospel values that Jesus taught?" Or if I'm furious with my boss, I ask for God's impression of the relationship: "Am I right to be angry, Lord? Am I being fair, here? Am I being unjustly treated? Is this argument worth fighting for? Or should I try to let this one go? Also, is there some fault of my own that I have not yet owned up to?"

3. I spend some time thanking God for the life of that person (even if my present feelings toward the person are very negative) and I ask God to help me to carry God's *own perception* of this person throughout my day. If I've made some decision about how to act today and feel that the action is the right thing to do, then I ask God to give me the courage to do what needs to be done.

Exercise U: Worthy Future Distractions

This exercise begins with the presumption that I am in the middle of my prayer time and am having trouble quieting myself because of some worthy distraction about a future event in my life, such as Friday's big test or tomorrow's big business meeting.

1. Once I have decided that this future happening is worth praying over, I change strategies and now focus on it. I ask God to show me the situation from his perspective: "Am I right to be concerned, happy, anxious? Do I have my priorities well placed? How can I promote gospel values through this future event?"

2. I ask God to show me the underlying values in this future event. If the event is the big test coming up, perhaps the value I will reflect on is my own education or the particular value of the subject matter itself. If the event is work related, perhaps the value is simply living out my vocation through the particular business at hand.

3. I ask God to help me see the spiritual pitfalls in the situation. "Could I be focusing too much or too little on my studies? Is this a fair and just business deal for all involved?" I ask God to show me what I can do to avoid these pitfalls and to give me the strength and courage to do what needs to be done.

4. I might want to close with one of the two prayers found at the end of Exercise Q in Chapter Seven.

CONCLUSION

Having distractions in my prayer is not a mark of inadequacy or inability. It simply means that I'm human. I need not worry about the various distractions that come and go, because God, the creator of my wandering spirit, will have no problems getting around and through them. He may even be the source of these distractions, calling me to refocus my prayerful attention on them.

NOTES

1. Thomas Merton, *New Seeds of Contemplation* (Norfolk, Conn.: New Directions, 1962).
2. Thomas H. Green, *When the Well Runs Dry* (Notre Dame, Ind.: Ave Maria Press, 1979), pp. 50-52.

chapter twelve

When I'm Bored with God
Dealing with Dryness

The previous chapter explained that I shouldn't worry about distractions that come and go in my prayer because they ultimately have little lasting impact. But at some point in my prayer life, I may go through a longer and much more difficult period, wherein my prayer simply dries up. I will receive no graces to enrich my life—no delightful and inspiring treasures floating to the surface. Instead, every prayer time will be filled with restlessness and/or boredom. The problem with dryness is not that something bad happens in prayer, but rather that nothing is happening at all. I just sit there by myself with no sign of the presence of God.

The vast majority of beginners quit praying at this point. Most do not consciously choose to stop praying; they just gradually pray a little less and a little less until one day, they look back and realize that they hardly pray at all anymore. Very seldom do they realize or admit that the reason they quit was because they got bored and lost interest. After all, who would admit—even to themselves—that they were bored with God? Instead, they simply convince themselves that they are just too busy right now and that they will return to it when things slow down (which never happens).

What is tragic about this problem is that this moment of dryness may well be the most momentous of my prayer life. Often, it is at this moment that God is inviting me to a much deeper and more mature relationship with him. Most beginners don't realize how close they are to something really big. All they know is the emptiness of the experience.

There are three possible causes of the experience of dryness: (1) It could be an external problem; (2) it could be a deeper spiritual problem; or (3) it could be God calling me to a very special period of growth, sometimes called *the desert experience*. If I have a spiritual director/mentor or a good friend with whom I can share my prayer experiences, the two of us can explore these possibilities together. It is difficult to figure them out on my own because the negative emotions that accompany this dry period might hamper my objectivity. Someone on the outside of the dryness will be able to help me keep the issues in proper perspective.

This chapter briefly explores these three possible causes, paying particular attention to the call of the desert (the third cause). The next chapter explores that calling even further by proposing a few metaphors that help to understand what might be happening in this strange and mysterious moment of my prayer life. It concludes with a few modest suggestions to help the beginner deal with (and maybe even thrive in) the desert.

Details, Details, Details

My dry period may be caused by some external problem. I may simply need to make a few adjustments in the details of how I pray. Here are a few considerations:

I consider my prayer space and body position. My place and position should be quiet and comfortable, but not so much that I fall asleep easily. Most people prefer a comfy straight-back chair (such as an armchair or a recliner) in a dimly lit room. But others find that lying flat on one's back, taking a walk or sitting in a lotus position on the floor works for them.

I consider the time of day when I pray. If I am too sleepy, hungry, energetic or preoccupied in the early morning, the time most people prefer, I can try the noon hour, the evening or even the late night hour.

I consider the prayer activities I am presently using. If I have been doing the same thing in my prayer for a while, perhaps I simply need to vary my activities. My job or schoolwork may be causing me "information overload," and I find myself uncontrollably analyzing Scripture in the same way I analyze whatever comes across my desk. If so, I try spending less of my prayer time reading and more of it simply sitting in the silence of God.

I consider my emotional state. Perhaps I am going through a stressful time at school or work or in one of my relationships. Anxiety or fatigue will make it very difficult to concentrate during prayer. Instead of fighting to forget it, I try to make that anxiety the focal point of the prayer. After all, God's desire is for me to be happy and healthy. I spend my prayer time telling God all about the problem and listening to God's response. If the anxiety is particularly intense and I feel that I need more time before facing it head-on, I take my mind off of it by temporarily doing more activities in my prayer. The repetition of a mantra or praying the rosary can often have a soothing affect.

WHO, ME?

If the problem is not external, then perhaps it is a spiritual problem. My prayer may be uncomfortable because it does not resonate with the way I am presently living my life. Maybe there is some unacknowledged sinful side of my life that is causing my soul to avoid God. Guilty children often blow their cover by their obvious state of discomfort in the presence of their parents. A priest walking through high school corridors will often have the same experience. If parents and priests can evoke such discomfort in guilty parties, how much more uncomfortable will our sinful souls be in the presence of our heavenly Father!

It is important to note that the problem is not about God's anger or wrath. God is not punishing me in my prayer time. The Father of Love does not play those games. The problem is my discomfort in the presence of such love. In the book of Exodus, the Lord looked down upon the Israelites and lovingly cared for them as they crossed the Red Sea. When the Egyptians pursued them, however, the Lord glanced at them and they found their chariots bogged down in the mud. They were paralyzed. When reading this story people often imagine that the loving gaze of God upon the Israelites was completely different from the powerful glance of God that stopped the Egyptians in their tracks. But I wonder if maybe God gave both peoples the same glance. It's just that the oppressive Egyptians were paralyzed in the face of such love (see Exodus 14:10-31).

Saint Ignatius says that for those living a Christ-like life, God's presence is as water on a sponge. Like the sponge, I effortlessly absorb God and am filled up by him. But for those in need of conversion, God's touch feels like the crashing of the ocean against the craggy coast.[1] Prayer is not pleasant because my soul is not in a condition to receive its graces. My cup of salvation will not overflow with the goodness and kindness of God, as in Psalm 23, because it is already filled with other gods, not nearly so good and kind. So this dry period in my prayer life may be a sort of wake-up call for me. If this is the case, I know what I need to do: "Repent, for the kingdom of heaven has come near" (Matthew 4:17).

JOURNEY INTO THE UNKNOWN

It could well be that the dryness does not come from anything exterior or through any fault of my own. In fact, the dryness may not be a problem at all but rather a calling from God for me to enter into a very special phase of my prayer life. God may be calling me into the desert. This experience is the subject of much of the writing of the mystics. Saint Thérèse of Lisieux, calling herself a little ball in the hand of the child Jesus, says of this experience, "Jesus pierced His little plaything; He wanted to see what there was inside it, and having seen, content with His discovery, He let His little ball fall to the ground and He went off to sleep."[2] Saint John of the Cross calls it "the dark night of the soul" and a present-day spiritual writer, Sister Ruth Burrows, calls it the "lights-off" experience. In this chapter, it will generally be referred to as the desert experience or as the experience of dryness.

A local Dallas radio station hosted a mystery vacation contest, wherein the winner was to show up at the airport packed and prepared for anything. In fact, she was not told where and what her vacation would be until the plane touched down at its destination. This is a good analogy of a person's prayer life. Each of us who embarks on a prayer life is beginning a unique mystery trip with God as our pilot. Your trip may be to a beautiful sandy beach, while mine may be to a dusty dude ranch. You may be climbing cold and treacherous mountains, while I dance with gorillas in a hot and humid jungle. Actually, it's even more wondrous than this. For each individual's prayer life contains within it a series of unique trips. Our prayer lives are as varied and complex as our real lives.

Within this diversity of prayer experiences, an occasional pray-er has practically always had an easy-going trip. Prayer for this person has generally always been a fishing excursion filled with exciting catches of divine grace. Many people assume that *anyone* who prays has this type of experience all the time. This is the experience many people expect to have when they begin a prayer life. After all, Jesus did say, "Ask, and it will be given you; search, and you will find; knock, and the door will be opened for you" (Matthew 7:7).

But the truth is that for most pray-ers, God has set a more unusual itinerary. In the midst of the great fishing trips and relaxing sandy beaches, God may sooner or later call me into the desert. Such a trip is not an easy one. It may demand a great deal of perseverance and stamina. Again, the length and breadth of this desert will vary greatly from one person to another. For some, the desert will be small and of little consequence, but for others— many others—the desert is unimaginably vast.

If I have been blessed by a calling into the desert (and yes, it is indeed a blessing), I will go through long periods when the trea- sure-filled waters dry up and I find myself sitting in my boat on a dry desert wasteland. No longer will I joyfully, peacefully bask in the consoling presence of God. There will be no sense of God's presence at all and I will begin to doubt if there ever was. I will call upon God to come and rescue me, and will be shocked when nothing happens. In place of God's presence will be a myriad of uncomfortable and unpleasant emotions: anger, fear, loneliness, restlessness, frustration, doubt and, most of all, boredom. I will be bored out of my mind. I will want to scream and run from the room. My once precious prayer space will be the last place I will want to visit. I will dread the coming of my daily prayer hour. I will lift the sofa cushions of my mind, searching for the Does It Count? game pieces I tossed away when I committed myself to prayer.[3]

Jesus must have gone through this painful experience as he endured the crucifixion. Some Christians believe that Jesus was all-knowing at all points of his life. But if he was "like us in all things but sin,"[4] then at least on some level, he had to know what it was like to stand alone in a fog of doubt and confusion. "My God, my God, why have you forsaken me?"[5] he cried out to his Father. It was this very darkness and confusion that made the crucifixion so painful for him.

CONCLUSION

So, despite my expectations, prayer may not always be a consoling and inspiring experience. There may be very difficult periods when it will be anything but that. These difficult periods are sometimes caused by exterior problems or by my own sinfulness. If so, there are things that I can do to fix the problem. But it may be that the problem is not a problem at all, but rather is a calling by God into the desert.

But why would God allow or even will for me to have such a difficult experience? This question is explored in the next chapter.

NOTES

1. *SpirEx*, 335.
2. *Story of a Soul: The Autobiography of St. Thérèse of Lisieux* (Washington, D.C.: ICS Publications, 1976), p. 136.
3. See "Calling and Commitment," Chapter One, p. 7.
4. CCC, #467. See also Hebrews 4:15.
5. Mark 15:34.

chapter thirteen

Why I'm Bored with God
Hints of an Explanation

'...my soul thirsts for you;
my flesh faints for you,
as in a dry and weary land where there is no water.'
—Psalm 63:1

Why would God let my prayer run dry? Why would God ever abandon me? Why would God not come when I cry out to him? What motivation could he possibly have for abandoning his child in my hour of need?

Please understand: *God never abandons his children.* I may go through times when it feels as though God is not present. But it is just that: a feeling. God is ever present in every atom of the universe. If he truly abandoned me for even a moment, I would cease to exist.

But if God loves me and is ever present, why would he ever allow me to even feel abandoned? Why does God call me into the desert at all? These are extremely difficult questions and will require a bit of explanation. It is the subject of this chapter.

In Search of Clues
The Book of Job teaches that it is impossible for me to step into God's shoes and figure out what his motives might be (see Job 38–42). I can, however, receive glimpses of the divine plan. I

can grasp hints of an explanation by observing the experience of human lives. Since we are made in God's image (see Genesis 1:27), I can study the "stuff" of ordinary human experience and make conjectures about what God may be up to. I can look to the creature for the mark of the Creator. This is what I must do as I reflect on why God might take me through this experience of dryness. I must look to some of the images of difficult moments in everyday life and use them to piece together the mystery of the spiritual desert.

Below, I propose four ways that experiences of everyday life reflect the experience of dryness in prayer. I present prayer as a mountain climb, a discipline, a relationship and as an experience of death and resurrection. By exploring these images, we can gain insight into why the difficult parts of my prayer might actually be the most important of all.

PRAYER IS A MOUNTAIN CLIMB

In a world of elevators and automated walkways, the number of mountain climbers keeps growing. Why would someone choose such an arduous task as a form of recreation? Imagine the straining fingers grasping for subtle indentations in the rock. As the days wear on, the climber's body must endure cuts, bruises, sprains, soreness and fatigue. Perhaps more difficult than all these are the dull steps, the uneventful reaches, the monotonous creeping. And through so much of it, the peak remains hidden in the clouds, seemingly out of reach.

Prayer is an uphill climb. It demands the type of spirit that chooses the difficult path—the road not usually taken. It involves hours and hours of slow and uneventful inching. And there are backslides, avalanches and hard falls. But somehow, like the mountain climber, I find meaning in it all—in the giant leaps and the mediocre inches. I even find meaning in getting up after a difficult spill and recovering lost ground. All of it, the peaks and the valleys—the plateaus and the cliffs—all are part of the adventure of prayer.

Prayer Is a Discipline

For every minute a professional athlete spends actually performing, she must spend hours and hours practicing. The ratio of practice to play time of a typical athlete is astounding. A soccer player, for example, spends untold hours in drilling, strategizing, weight training and exercising before enjoying the fleeting minutes of the game. And even then, the average player spends precious few of those minutes actually on the field. Any player who is in the sport for the glory of it will not last; there are simply too many inglorious hours.

Likewise, a professional musician spends countless hours alone in his room laboriously practicing one small but difficult piece of the music he hopes to perform someday. Imagine how many awkward and ugly sounds come from that instrument before that one glorious moment when the noise becomes music. Furthermore, for both the athlete and the musician, the ratio of tiresome practice to exciting performance does not change with time or experience. On the contrary, the professionals are those willing to endure an even harsher regimen.

When I pray, I am in training for the greatest event of all—the moment when my soul returns to its Maker and the two become one again. As difficult as the training may be for a great sport or a grand musical performance, it cannot compare to the training required for this Main Event. For this is a most unusual training: I am training not to overcome, but to surrender—not to perform, but to stop doing and allow the Other to do all. As Thomas Green says, "I am learning to float, not to swim."[1]

This letting go feels unnatural at times. To allow anyone, even God, to possess my mind, body and will requires relinquishing the very control I spend my life pursuing. Through the many hours of restless and emotionless prayer, my body learns to be still, my mind learns to slow itself down and my soul learns submission to its Creator. That is why the training must be long and arduous at times. And throughout the pray-er's lifetime, the Lord demands an ever-greater surrendering, which, as in the case of the professional athlete or the virtuoso, may demand an increasingly more intense regimen.

Prayer Is a Relationship

Various relationships in life resemble my relationship with God. For example, God can be my parent, spouse, teacher or friend.

God is my parent. A pray-er demanding constant ecstatic and extraordinary experiences from God is like a child on a diet of pure sweets. Like candy, these moments are not what bring about the most growth in me. During the difficult times, God comes to me as a competent and challenging mother who says to her child, "Yes, I do have more lollipops in my purse, but I love you and want you to grow up strong and healthy. So I will not give you another one, no matter how much you cry."

Mom is also the one who teaches me to walk. A pray-er in dry prayer is like a baby feeling abandoned by Mom, as Mom backs up with every painfully new step he takes toward her. Is it cruel of the mother to back away from her lurching child? On the contrary, this distancing is evidence of her great love. Likewise, if I were able to transcend my limited perspective, I would understand the Great Mother's love as I take my lonely steps toward her.

Sometimes children grow impatient when their wise parents do not allow them to grow up too fast. The child's frustration is actually a good sign because it reveals his yearning to become an adult. Likewise, the ache of a dry prayer time may well be this same wonderful yearning to grow up. I remember, while on one of my first retreats, I spent several days asking God to place me at the foot of the cross. I wanted to witness the crucifixion as I had never done before. Days went by and nothing happened. Finally, one day, I asked God, "Why won't you show me the cross?" God responded by reminding me of something my uncle Leland once said about his childhood. He said that only as an adult did he realize why his mother sometimes would not eat with the family. Sometimes, there simply was not enough food to go around and she secretly had to settle for the scraps that were left over. In my prayer, God showed me an image of my uncle and my father as happy (and well-fed) children, blissfully ignorant of their mother's sacrifices to make them so. God then said to me, "This is why I don't show you the cross. You're not ready for it yet." Sometimes God does not send us a particular grace (like the grace of seeing Jesus on the cross), because he knows that we are just not ready for such an experience yet.

God is my teacher. I remember one long, hot Dallas afternoon when one of my students had to stay after school to do an assignment for me. This difficult pupil was not my biggest fan to begin with and my forcing him to stay after school for the umpteenth time did not help my approval ratings. But on this particular afternoon, when the school was practically empty and the two of us wearily and begrudgingly trudged on with our work, a bond seemed to form between the two of us. Subconsciously, I think each of us appreciated the other's efforts (feeble though they were) to cooperate, despite all of our desires not to do so. It was because of the unpleasantness of the situation that we appreciated each other's presence. Had we both enjoyed staying after school, there would have been no sacrifice required.

Likewise, when I look back on my prayer life, it was in the long and arduous moments—when God and I struggled desperately to understand and to make ourselves understood—that we grew closer to one another. It was in these moments when I didn't want to be there but was there anyway, that a special bond between God and me developed.

God is my spouse. It seems to me that what distinguishes a strong and secure marriage from a weak and fragile one is not the exuberant or passionate moments. Everyone who falls in love experiences these. What makes the lasting relationship so strong is how they deal with the hard times. Every marriage has its moments when the last place each of them wants to be is at the spouse's side. And yet, in the enduring relationship, that is where they will be. I'm sure that even the staid Savoys[2] have had moments in their lives when one or the other wanted so badly to walk off that porch, never to return. But each draws strength from the assurance that, until death parts them, the other will be at the lover's side, regardless of fleeting emotions.

Sometimes I feel bored with my Heavenly Spouse, too. Sometimes other porches seem more attractive. I think that God allows me to feel bored at times in order to give me the opportunity to give that gift of spousal sacrifice back to God. I may even have to say, "God, I've really been bored and restless in prayer lately. No offense, but I don't feel like being here today. I'm not going anywhere, though. I'm committed to you, Lord. So while on the surface I may not feel like being here, deeper down, there is nothing I want more than to love and be loved by you." These opportunities for fidelity deepen and enrich my relationship with God.

God is my friend. Friendship also requires great sacrifice at times. A few years ago, while on my annual retreat, I spent five long days in desolate prayer as dry as the Sahara. No matter how much I begged Jesus to come out and play, I sat alone in my little wagon, filled with sadness and self-pity. On the sixth day, I meditated on Mark 4:35-41, where the disciples, out of fear of the weather, rouse Jesus from deep sleep. In my prayer, I imagined myself as one of those frightened disciples, watching Jesus begin to fall asleep just as the storms within me are beginning to brew. "Mark, you've been my friend through good times and bad," he said. "You were there when I fed the masses and you were there when I fled from the mobs. I know you will also be at my side in the dramatic moments yet to come. You will even stand at the foot of my cross and hold my mother while I die. But I have a special request for you right now. Will you sit by my side while I sleep?" Only then did I understand the meaning of the past five days. God was allowing me to be his faithful, self-sacrificing friend. With a greater fidelity, I could now pray the antiphon from the Liturgy of the Hours, "My joy is to remain with you, my God" (Vol. 2, page 1515).

There is a common strand in the images presented thus far. All of them imply that there is great value in self-sacrifice. The relationship images in particular seem to indicate that this sacrifice may be a necessary element of mature, intimate relationships. Perhaps this is what God is up to when he allows dryness in my prayer: God sets up a situation that allows me to make a sacrifice for our relationship, thereby strengthening the bond between us. This calling to self-sacrifice is the very same calling to selflessness discussed in Chapter Three, "From Martha to Mary." The next (and last) image speaks more explicitly about this selflessness. But first, I present a concrete example of how I might pray during this period of dryness.

Exercise V: At the Side of a Sleeping Friend

This exercise presumes that I have been in the midst of a long period of dryness.

1. I begin the prayer with one of the solitude exercises found in Chapter Four. If possible, I relax in the stillness and the quiet for a while.

2. If and when I am ready, I slowly read Mark 4:35-41. I try to imagine what happened just before this scene. That is, I imagine myself as one of the disciples in the boat pushing away from shore so as to cross over to the other side. The farther we get from the shore, the more furious the wind gets.

3. In my imagination I notice that, though the ride is rough because of the ensuing storm, Jesus is so tired that he just can't keep his eyes open anymore. So I walk over to him and say, "It's OK, Lord. I will sit by your side as you sleep."

4. I make that statement my mantra, repeating it over and over again. I try to imagine myself sitting by the side of Jesus as he sleeps. Though my spiritual storm grows more furious, I am not concerned. Instead, I look with love on my friend and Lord, keeping still so as not to wake him.

Prayer Is an Experience of Death and Resurrection

[I]t is no longer I who live, but it is Christ who lives in me.
—Galatians 2:20

A recurrent theme of the Old Testament tells me that I, as a mortal, cannot look upon the face of God and live (see Exodus 23:13-23).

The vision would simply be too much for me. It would blow my circuits. Sister Ruth Burrows uses this notion to explain the experience of dryness. In prayer, God slowly transforms me into an ever-new creation. I cannot become someone new, however, until my old self dies. "[U]nless a grain of wheat falls into the earth and dies, it remains just a single grain; but if it dies, it bears much fruit," says Jesus (John 12:24). If this is true, then these dry periods may, in fact, be the most important moments of my prayer life. For it is in these times that God is doing his mightiest work within me. These painful periods are as essential to my prayer life as the Crucifixion is to the salvation story.

Part of the reason this death is so painful is that it is a death to self. The mystics describe union with God as an experience of becoming lost in the presence of God. God and I become one, so much so that I am no longer sure where "I" ends and God begins. But in order for the "I" to be lost in God, I must first become wholly selfless. Like gold that is tested in fire, I must allow God to slowly burn away the parts of me that are not of God. The problem is that I have grown quite attached to these parts. Like crutches for a lame man, these parts of me artificially prop me up when I am feeling weak in the knees. These difficult prayer experiences sometimes feel like the crutches have been pulled away from me.

In this purification process, the first to go are my emotions. It is not that my emotions are bad, but they must be deactivated in order for me to begin to turn my focus from myself to God. If I still judge my prayer times by how much they bring me joy and happiness, then I still have not yet become selfless.

In my prayer life, I move to a place where what happens to the self is no longer my primary concern. According to Greek legend, the god Narcissus became transfixed, pined away and died when he saw his own reflection on the surface of the pond. He found himself so beautiful that he could not turn his eyes from the reflection. What happens in prayer is the opposite of this phenomenon. When I finally painfully turn my eyes away from my own reflection and look upon the face of God, I am so struck by *God's* beauty that I never look upon myself again. For all intents and purposes, the self no longer exists. This is what is meant by the Old Testament notion that upon looking at the face of God, we die.

This last explanation may be confusing. Words fail when speaking of this phenomenon, because it cannot be communicated in language. For those who have experienced it, it is too deep to explain adequately and for those who have never experienced it, it is too foreign to understand. All that is important for me to know right now is that these dry periods are part of the salvific plan of God. During these difficult periods, I must trust that God is present and active even when I do not feel anything. I must adopt the creed of the popular Catholic song of the 1970s:

> I believe in the sun,
> even when it isn't shining;
> I believe in love,
> even when there's no one there.
> And I believe in God,...
> even when He is silent.[3]

WHICH WAY TO THE BEACH?

OK, so now I have a better perspective on what may be going on in my trip through the desert. But the question remains, "Which way to the beach?" I know now that prayer, at times, can be as fatiguing as football, but I still don't even know where the end zone is. How might I come to some resolution in this challenging desert experience?

If the experience has not been going on for very long, I may simply be going through a brief spell that will ease up after a while. My novice master, Father Fran Pistorius, used to say, "If you're traveling through the desert and a sandstorm begins to brew, get off your horse, lie face down in the sand and wait it out." If I am going through a difficult period in prayer and have done all I can to improve it, then all I can do is *"wait it out."* It'll blow over eventually and I'll be the better for the experience. This, by the way, is another time when a good spiritual director or mentor can be invaluable.[4] He or she will be able to stand outside the storm and assure me that good weather is on the way.

Another strategy is to wrestle with God for the blessing of his presence in the way that Jacob wrestled with the angel (see Genesis 32:23-31). This again seems to be a natural if not healthy phase in any relationship. When friends survive a really rough spot in their friendship, they usually end up having a stronger bond because of it.

The Old Testament is filled with extraordinary passages wherein the hero of the story confronts God and calls him to keep his promise of steadfastness toward his people. These passages are great for praying over when I am going through long periods of dryness. Here are a few examples:

> Look down from heaven and see, / from your holy and
> glorious habitation. / Where are your zeal and your might?
> / The yearning of your heart and your compassion? They
> are withheld from me.... O that you would tear open the
> heavens and come down,/so that the mountains would
> quake at your presence— ....Your holy cities have become

a wilderness,/Jerusalem a desolation.... After all this, will you restrain yourself, O Lord? Will you keep silent, and punish us so severely? (Isaiah 63:15; 64:1, 10, 12)

In spite of everything let us give thanks to the Lord our God, who is putting us to the test as he did our ancestors. Remember what he did with Abraham, and how he tested Isaac, and what happened to Jacob in Syrian Mesopotamia, while he was tending the sheep of Laban, his mother's brother. For he has not tried us with fire, as he did them, to search their hearts, nor has he taken vengeance on us; but the Lord scourges those who are close to him in order to admonish them. (Judith 8:25-27)

I stretch out my hands to you;/my soul thirsts for you like a parched land. Answer me quickly, O Lord; my spirit fails./Do not hide your face from me, or I shall be like those who go down to the Pit. (Psalm 143:6-7)

My God, my God, why have you forsaken me?/Why are you so far from helping me, from the words of my groaning? O my God, I cry by day, but you do not answer; and by night, but find no rest. (Psalm 22:1-2)

CALLED TO BE A BEDOUIN?

Now here's the absolutely scariest statement of the whole book: Sometimes the storm lasts a long, long time. God calls some of his children to make their dwelling in the dry desert lands of passionless prayer. I know that this may be hard for me to accept right now, but I may never see the ocean again. I may never feel the joy, fervor and passion I felt as a "baby pray-er" when God spoonfed me everything. And yet, is this really bad news? Do I really wish to leave solid food behind and return to strained carrots? Growing up is tough and demanding. But it's rewarding, too. Kids are always looking upon the seemingly drab lives of adults and wanting to run away to Never-Never Land, but do I, as an adult, really want to go through childhood again?

Recently, a friend and I were speaking about prayer. It seems that she had not been able to sustain a vivid and lively prayer life. She wanted to know what she needed to do to fix it so that it might better match what she always expected prayer should be like. Later, as we moved on to other topics, I told her how impressed I was by the obvious love her husband and she had for one another after so many years of marriage. She responded:

Yes, Jim and I could not be happier together. We're a perfect fit. You know, the longer we live together, the more I appreciate the little things. Take yesterday, for instance. I spent hours here in the kitchen cooking and baking while he spent the afternoon on the computer, plodding through our taxes. At one point, while waiting for the pasta water to boil and the chicken to finish baking, I made a quick cup of hot cocoa and brought it up to him. His furrowed face didn't turn from the numbers on the screen, but I saw him smile a little as he pretended not to watch me lay the cup down next to his keyboard. Without a word exchanged between us, I kissed him on the forehead and walked out of the room. That moment is as precious to me as the passionate moments in our marriage.

I was touched by that story and told her so. I then asked her if she appreciated ordinary moments in her relationship with God as much. She immediately understood what I was trying to say. In search of the passionate moments of prayer, she had missed out on all of the ordinary ones.

What a beautiful love these two shared, and yet, would a kid pay full price to see this hot cocoa scene on the big screen? Only those who have been in a relationship for a while will understand how fulfilling such an everyday moment with one's lover can be. In the same way, when novice pray-ers imagine a prayer life with few extraordinary experiences, they sometimes shudder in fear. But after living in the desert a while, an experienced pray-er will find it teeming with life.

What I am saying is that instead of gradually moving out of this dry experience of prayer, I may eventually let go of the need for ecstatic experiences and begin to "draw water from the dry well," as Thomas H. Green puts it. The desert doesn't change, but I do. This is the irony of the experience: it is only when I give up on finding the way out of the desert that my insatiable thirst is quenched.

Conclusion

I had a dream once...

...that I had just died and was at Dallas/Fort Worth airport, which was filled with other recently deceased people all waiting to catch their plane to heaven. It seems the plane would be late and that we were all to fulfill certain tasks before boarding. It was sort of like a scavenger-hunt, whereby we all had to walk through security, get our shoes shined, purchase a newspaper, buy a sandwich and so on.

At each stop, I happily conversed with the personnel. At security, we laughed together about the age and condition of my luggage. At the shoeshine stand, we grieved over the Rangers' recent loss. And at the sandwich shop, I teasingly asked if a Lexus came with the price of my tuna sandwich.

At each place there were a few fellow travelers who joined in the fun, but most nervously watched the second hand of their watches. At the lunch counter, one particularly uptight man failed to see the humor in my Lexus joke. As he grudgingly gave up his sandwich money, he asked the clerk how a plane from heaven could possibly be late. That exasperating question struck the clerk and me as hilarious and the two of us split our sides laughing.

As time went on and we continued about our menial tasks, it slowly began to dawn on me that *there was no plane—that this, in fact, was our final destination.* And that whether you were in heaven or hell was entirely dependent on your sense of humor or lack thereof.

For whatever reason, God at times allows me to go through long periods of dryness in my prayer. Like the anxious man in the sandwich shop, I often grow impatient with God because he does not take me to a place that *I* consider heavenly. But if I can quiet my fretful spirit enough to accept and embrace the place he *has* taken me to, I may find God even in the midst of nothingness. I may even begin to find life in this place that is free of emotions, images and pleasant experiences—devoid of everything but God and me.

Notes

1. *When the Well Runs Dry*, pp. 142ff.
2. See Chapter Three.
3. "I Believe in the Sun," words and music by Rev. Carey Landry, North American Liturgy Resources, 1973.
4. See Chapter Ten.

chapter fourteen

STAGE FOUR—BEING WITH GOD
Contemplative Prayer

I have reserved the fourth and final stage of prayer for near the end of the book because it is this stage that is the objective for the whole adventure of contemplative prayer. All of my efforts in prayer are to arrive at this place. To describe it, then, is to define prayer itself. Although not the last chapter, this chapter will serve as a sort of overview of much of which I have been speaking. Specifically, I define prayer as recognition of God, transformation by God and union with God.

THE STILL POINT

Earlier, I called this stage "the Mary-state-of-being" because it is here that I, like both biblical Marys, abandon all of my activity (what I have called "the Martha-state-of-doing") and sit before the Lord with empty hands and open heart. I embody receptivity. I do so because at this stage, God has finally become my all and there is no longer any need to self-initiate anything in prayer. Like our spiritual mother, Mary, "My soul magnifies the Lord" (Luke 1:47; see also 1:46-55).

When speaking of prayer to his brother priests, Cardinal Joseph Bernardin said that prayer leads the pray-er to "the soul...that still-point at the heart of every person, that deepest center, that point of encounter with the transcendent yet incarnate Mystery of God."

I like to think of prayer as a microcosm of all that I call, "Mark." The origins of the word *microcosm* are from the Greek words *micros*, meaning "small," and *kosmos*, meaning "world, universe or cosmos." Prayer then is the small universe where all the stuff of me exists—the good and the bad, the ecstasies and the agonies of my life. This state of being is as close as I can come to the core of my very self—the essence of my existence. It is the zygote of me, that which existed before all else and from which my life has sprung.

In a way, I, as a pray-er am like an astronomer trying to understand the entire universe I call "me" by visiting that "place" where the Big Bang first banged. Once I do understand it, it is here in this place that my universe must be re-centered. My worlds must be put back on their proper axes, orbiting around the true Son. For what happens here at this micro-cosmos—this epicenter of my creation—ripples through all of my existence. This re-centering is actually a re-perceiving, for God was, is and always will be God. What is in need of repair, then, is the blindness that keeps me from understanding my divine origins and from experiencing God as the universe wherein my star shines.

PRAYER IS RECOGNITION OF GOD

In trying to explain how God communicates, Saint Ignatius said, "God works and labors for me in all creatures upon the face of the earth."[1] In other words, God's answers to my deepest questions do not need to be given to me in prayer because they are already embedded in creation. The trick, then, is not to get God to answer me during that prayer time, but rather to allow God to teach me how to perceive the answers that have been around me all along. That is what prayer does. It disposes me to hear God's voice in the ordinary moments of my day. When I pray, therefore,

I should not ask, "God, give me a sign," but rather, "God, give me sight," because this is what I really lack. When God asks, "What do you want me to do for you?" I should answer as Bartimaeus answered that question, "Let me see again" (Mark 10: 51).

I love a car with character. I used to drive a fifteen-year-old Chevy Citation. It was rusty and dented and its pleasant purr had long ago become a deep moan. One day while driving on the interstate with the windows rolled down and the radio cranked up, the car began to have a strange feel to it. I turned the radio down and heard an ominous clatter coming from the front of the car. Unfortunately, except for the location of the brake and the gas pedal, I know nothing about cars. So I tried to solve the problem by using the oldest psychological trick in the book: denial. I turned the radio louder and pretended I heard nothing. But instead of bobbing my head to the beat of the music, I found myself keeping time with the rhythm of the rattle. The clatter had not gotten any louder, but my ears were now inescapably attuned to its forbidding cadence. I realized I would get no peace until I heeded its woeful cry.

The reverberation beneath the hood in my Chevy story can be likened to the sound of God's voice calling me to conversion long before I even begin to listen for it. The music from the radio is the noise of my everyday incredibly busy life. The process of prayer is the act of turning down the noise of the world (the radio) in order to hear the voice of God (the sound beneath the hood). But here's the important part of the story: When I turned the radio up to loud again, *I was still able to hear the sound*, not because it had gotten any louder, but because I had now become *attuned* to it. In the same way, when I leave my prayer time and return to my noisy life, I can still hear the Lord's voice because my prayer has made me attuned to it.

Spiritual writers often say things like, "God speaks in the rustle of the leaves and the songs of the birds." I would say that God goes even further than that. God speaks not only through the beauty of nature, but also through every atom of creation and in every moment of time; from bees to buildings, from trees to TV's, God labors through the elements to tell me of his love. When I am in need of answers from God, then prayer becomes a means of giving God permission to fine-tune the spiritual senses of my soul so that I might recognize the God of Wisdom who lies in wait for me at the dinner table, on the freeway, at work, in the classroom, at the movies and anywhere else I might find myself on a given day.

The cynics will say, "That's all in your head. The tree is just a tree and the birdsong is just birdsong. God is nowhere." Imagine driving down the road and reading such a sign: GodIsNowhere

Think of that sign as a symbol of the world. The cynics look at this world and see nothing sacred or divine, only molecules of matter. GOD IS NOWHERE. But to those who have allowed God to fine-tune their spiritual senses, the world is shouting GOD IS NOW HERE! Note that both are looking at the exact same thing, and yet what they *perceive* is entirely different.

I remember as a teacher attending a track meet one bright and sunny day, wearing cheap yellow sunglasses. At one point I walked up to the water cooler, pushed the nozzle and put my hands under the trickle. One of my students was alarmed and asked, "Mr. Thibs, what are you doing?" I said, "I'm just washing my hands." He responded, "But in Gatorade!?" The Gatorade was yellow, but because of my sunglasses, everything in my world was yellow that day! My lenses distorted my perception of reality. When I pray, the Lord gives me lenses that do the opposite. They restore and clarify my perception of reality.

The experience is like looking at one of those unusual 3-D grainy pictures on display at any mall. At first glance, it reveals nothing, just a bunch of dots. But if I stand quietly and focus well, amazing images begin to appear. Once I finally see this new world beneath the surface, I will say, "Wow, I can't believe I didn't see it from the start." If I turn away for a minute and then return to it, this new world will instantly reappear. In fact, now that I have become acclimated to it, I cannot *not* see the image beneath the surface. If someone were to say, "It's all in your head, there's nothing here but dots," I will have no way to prove otherwise. All I can do is encourage her to stand still and quiet for a moment and really *look* at the picture. In the same way, I cannot prove to my cynic friend that God's voice is present in every ordinary moment of the day. Besides giving a few pointers, all I can do is encourage her to sit still a moment and really *listen*. Maybe she'll hear it, too.

As discussed in Chapters Seven and Eight, "Listening to God" and "Reading the Signs of the Prayer Times," God does indeed talk back during my prayer times. But over the years, I have learned that what God says to me in prayer is not as important as the ability prayer gives me to hear God's voice in my everyday life, in every person, and at all times. When I am in the stage of Listening to God, I am about the task of hearing God's voice in prayer. When I move to the stage of Being with God, I continue to listen, but now I am listening to God's silence. Through this process of listening, precisely when God is silent, I dispose myself to hear his voice everywhere. In other words, if I can grow to hear God in the silence, then I can hear and see and taste and smell and touch God in everything.

PRAYER IS TRANSFORMATION BY GOD

There is a wonderful scene in the movie *Shadowlands*, in which the cancer-burdened wife of C.S. Lewis receives good news from her doctor. A friend joyfully says to C.S., "I know how hard you've been praying—and now God is answering your prayer." But C.S. responds, "That's not why I pray, Harry. I pray because I can't help myself.... It doesn't change God. It changes me."[2] By this stage in my prayer life, I realize that prayer is not about what things God does for me, countless as they are, but about the transformation God causes within me because of prayer. God brings me to this stage of solitude and nothingness so that my focus might shift from what is going on inside prayer to what is happening inside me. In the earlier stages of my prayer life, my concern is *what* comes out of my prayer. In this final stage, my concern is *who* comes out of my prayer.

Prayer, then, transforms my life from the inside out. Earlier I said that I, as a human, tend to be entrenched in the Martha-state-of-doing. I place great value on what I do and little on who I am. In fact, I generally operate out of the assumption that my identity (who I am) is determined by my actions (what I do). When I don't like myself, I try to become a different person by changing my actions. But contemplative pray-ers operate out of the assumption that my actions spring forth from the kind of person I am, not the other way around. In order to transform myself then, I must go to the source. This computer problem is serious enough to open up the main frame.

How does this happen in the stage of Being with God? By daily sitting in the nothingness of this prayer—not seeking answers, consolations, good feelings or anything else from God—by just sitting with open arms, I learn to submit to God. I begin to allow God to be my God, not for the favors he might bestow on me, but because of the love he has for me. And it doesn't just happen in my prayer time. My ever deeper surrendering in that core of my being will spring forth a whole life of surrendering to God. When I leave that state of being and return to my daily activities, I do so with a whole new disposition. Only now am I disposed to God's lordship in every moment and every aspect of life.

Earlier, I explored the question of why would God call me into the desert of desolation. I see now that my human condition will cause me to manipulate any *thing* that is before me. Only in nothingness can I begin to surrender my own grossly inadequate lordship to the true King. This experience of nothingness, of the desert that I dreaded, feared and loathed in my young prayer life, turns out to be an all-important moment in the slow process of my own transformation.

PRAYER IS UNION WITH GOD

Throughout this book, I have tried to explain things as concretely as possible. Using stories and examples, I have tried to spell out for the reader the sometimes-ambiguous concepts of the experience of contemplative prayer. But when it comes to speaking of the union with God one experiences in this final stage, all words seem to falter. No description seems to get at the overwhelming sense of God and me *as one*. The best that one can do to understand this phenomenon is to recall the most intimate moment of one's past, when one felt most connected with another person—a time similar to my last days with Aunt Sally:

> ...But as the days turned into months we spoke much less. Whole days would go by in almost complete silence. Looking back on my life with Aunt Sally, it is the memory of those silent days that I now hold dear. I can't say how or why, but somehow those were the days when we were closest to one another, as though we had come to realize that the words we spoke simply crowded the room, like

> unwanted guests. The silence on the other hand pulled us
> closer together like a sacred cord that bonded us in ways
> beyond our control or understanding....

Those who have had such an experience will know what I mean when I say that it is a transcendent one. That is, it goes beyond any ordinary experience. It cannot be communicated to a third party because it is indescribable. It is not from the realm where words are formed. To understand it, one must experience it. Even the great spiritual writers seemed to lack the ability to fully express what they experienced at this stage. When they get to this part of their writing on prayer, they begin to fumble the words—to become awkward and clumsy with their allusions and examples.

Those who have had such an experience also know that I do not exit it untouched. The imprint of the other is permanently burned into my heart, so that I can never really leave that other again. In a sense, I, alone, no longer make up a complete whole. Perhaps this is what the story of Eve being created with the rib of Adam touches on (see Genesis 2:21-24). Adam is no longer whole without Eve. A part of him dwells in her. This is what the experience of Being With God feels like. And somehow, it seems as though God feels it too: "I will not forget you. See, I have inscribed you on the palms of my hands" (Isaiah 49:15b-16a).

The outflow of Being with God is, in a way, more extraordinary and more important than the experience itself. That I experience God in this most intimate way *during prayer* is astonishing. But even more so is the subsequent union I feel with God *in my everyday life*. Earlier I said that God speaks through buildings and bees, trees and TV's. That truth alone is extraordinary. But there is even more to it than that: I not only hear God in this stuff of my day, I *experience* him there. And what is more: I do not experience him extrinsically—outside of myself. I experience the God within me leaping for joy at himself inside that bee. It is the fetal John the Baptist within Elizabeth's womb, stirred in the presence of what dwelt inside Mary (see Luke 1:39-45).

Conclusion: Three in One

So then, when I pray I become attuned to the presence of God in my everyday life (recognition of God). I also begin to surrender all of my life to God's lordship during prayer (transformation by God). Finally, when I pray I come into mystical union with God, a oneness not severed when I rise from my prayer time (union with God). These are the three most important qualities of prayer.

Note, however, that the three are really one and the same quality. The transformation that takes place in prayer is ultimately a transformation of perception. What is surrendered in this transformation—my lordship and my separateness from God—never really existed in the first place. They were only illusions and mirages, smoke and mirrors. God has always been God and has always carried me in his bosom (see Isaiah 40:11). From the moment of my creation, God and I have always been together in mystical oneness. I just didn't know it until now.

And all of us, with unveiled faces, seeing the glory of the Lord as though reflected in a mirror [recognition], *are being transformed into the same image* [union] *from one degree of glory to another...* (2 Corinthians 3:18)

Notes

1. *SpirEx*, 236.
2. *Shadowlands*, Savoy Pictures, 1993.

Being with God

- **It is sometimes referred to as:** mystical union, pure contemplation, beatific vision.

- **Basically it is:** sitting in stillness, happily lost in God.

- **Some analogies include:** the oneness of the marital union, the transcendent qualities of true friendship, a nursing child at rest in his mother's arms (see Psalm 131).

- **The advantages of this type of prayer are:** It is the experience of intimate relationship with God; it is as close as one might come in this life to tasting heaven.

- **The distortion of this type of prayer is:** quietism. (See Chapter Fifteen for explanation.)

- **The transition to the next level might come when:** we die and experience the resurrection of body and soul.

chapter fifteen

PUTTING PRAYER IN ACTION
The Test of Authentic Prayer

Those who say, "I love God," and
hate their brothers or sisters, are liars.
—1 John 4:20

The previous chapter explained that the purpose of prayer is (a) to recognize God's presence, (b) to be transformed through surrendering to God's lordship and (c) to experience union with God. But these experiences of prayer must be concretized in order to be authentic. I should not be satisfied with a merely spiritual understanding of these graces. The graces of my prayer must be incarnated into the stuff of this world—interwoven into the fabric of my everyday life. I must ask myself, "Concretely, how have the recognition, transformation and union of my recent prayer been lived out in my family, my work, my studies, my play and so on?"

The graces of a healthy prayer life will reverberate in the actions of my everyday life. I throw a stone into a quiet pond. The stone is small and the spot it touches on the surface of the water is, too. And yet its ripples expand to every corner of the lake. From that tiny spot where the rock first made contact, waves are born and are carried to the very edges. In the same way, the effects of my short period of intimate contact with God will ripple through to the very edges of my day.

Many people do not understand this basic connection between their prayer lives and their everyday lives. They understand prayer as a way of separating the pray-er from the world. Prayer for them is a way of running away from the world and into the arms of God. But this is a terrible misunderstanding. For where would the world be except in the loving embrace of God? The Bible warns time and again against the fallacy that holds that I can be close to God without being close to God's people. It condemns any sort of God-and-me spirituality that does not result in an outpouring of love toward others:

Is such the fast that I choose,
a day to humble oneself?
Is it to bow down the head like a bulrush,
and to lie in sackcloth and ashes?
Will you call this a fast,
a day acceptable to the Lord?
Is not this the fast that I choose:
to loose the bonds of injustice,
to undo the thongs of the yoke,
to let the oppressed go free,
and to break every yoke?
Is it not to share your bread with the hungry,
and bring the homeless poor into your house;
when you see the naked, to cover them,
and not to hide yourself from your own kin? (Isaiah 58:5-7)

Jesus, too, does not mince words when admonishing pray-ers:
"Thus you will know them by their fruits."

"Not everyone who says to me, 'Lord, Lord,' will enter the kingdom of heaven, but the one who does the will of my Father in heaven. On that day many will say to me, 'Lord, Lord, did we not prophesy in your name, and cast out demons in your name, and do many deeds of power in your name?' Then I will declare to them, 'I never knew you....'" (Matthew 7:20-23)

...neither is Saint Paul "soft" on this issue:

If I speak in the tongues of mortals and of angels, but do not have love, I am a noisy gong or a clanging cymbal. And if I have prophetic powers, and understand all mysteries and all knowledge, and if I have all faith, so as to remove mountains, but do not have love, I am nothing. (1 Corinthians 13:1-2)

...nor is Saint James:

What good is it, my brothers and sisters, if you say you have faith but do not have works? Can faith save you? If a brother or sister is naked and lacks daily food, and one of you says to them, "Go in peace; keep warm and eat your fill," and yet you do not meet their bodily needs, what is the good of that? So faith by itself, if it has no works, is dead. (James 2:14-17)

This exclusive attitude wherein one pursues a life of prayer apart from a life of love and service has always been a serious problem. The frequency with which we find it mentioned throughout the Bible indicates just how serious it is. This mindset was even condemned by the Church as a heresy called *quietism*. It is another manifestation of my doggy-tail-chase described in Chapter Three. The human condition will sneak back into my prayer life, whispering into my ear, "Aren't you wonderful? What a saint you are!" Using my own prayerful acts as evidence, I will begin to believe that I am holier than the riffraff of the Church and stand alone with Christ above the sea of hypocrites and heathens that call themselves Christian. In disdain, I will look down on the world from my lofty position and thank God that I am not like these sinners.

Beginners in prayer are particularly susceptible to this distortion of the contemplative life. They can become so pleased with their newfound spiritual life that pride creeps in and poisons their spirit without their even being aware of it. It is a tricky problem and is extremely difficult to detect in oneself. This is why I have said that one of the three most important aspects of prayer is that of transformation to God's lordship—of increasingly becoming selfless. But even in receiving this grace from God, I can become prideful: "See how selfless I've become now that I'm such a great pray-er!"

I must do all I can to guard against this spiritual gangrene, which will eat away at my soul if I let it. Three important practices can help. First, I should pray unceasingly for the gift of humility and loving reverence for all of God's people. Second, as previously mentioned, I should seek out wise friends and mentors to challenge my prideful tendencies. Finally, I should spend a little time daily reflecting on my day, searching for the evidence of transformation in my life or the lack thereof. At the end of the day, I must look back on my actions and non-actions, my words and my moments of silence and ask myself, "Where is the fruit of my tree of prayer?" Saint Ignatius calls this type of reflection "The Examen" and insists that it is as important as, or more important than, my prayer time itself.[1] There is no better way to evaluate the authenticity of my prayer life.

So, using the three goals of prayer previously discussed, union, transformation and recognition, I look back on my day seeking the fruit of my prayer.

Prayer Is Union with God

Saint Paul says that we Christians are to be "ambassadors for Christ" (2 Corinthians 5:20). We are to be Christ's hands and Christ's feet until he comes again in glory. The mark of a true Christian, then, is not how much he or she prays, but rather how this mission of being Christ in the world is lived out.

Jesus says:

"When the Son of Man comes in his glory, and all the angels with him, then he will sit on the throne of his glory. All the nations will be gathered before him, and he will separate people one from another as a shepherd separates the sheep from the goats, and he will put the sheep at his right hand and the goats at the left. Then the king will say to those at his right hand, 'Come, you that are blessed by my Father, inherit the kingdom prepared for you from the foundation of the world; for I was hungry and you gave me food, I was thirsty and you gave me something to drink, I was a stranger and you welcomed me, I was naked and you gave me clothing, I was sick and you took care of me, I was in prison and you visited me....' 'Truly, I tell you, just as you did it to one of the least of these who are members of my family, you did it to me.'" (Matthew 25:31-40)

So often I spiritualize this and similar passages as a way of justifying the fact that I do not, in fact, feed the hungry, visit the sick and imprisoned and clothe the naked. I soothe my uncomfortable conscience by saying to myself, "Well, I prayed for the homeless today, so I am with them in spirit." Or, "Well, I wrote a check to Catholic Charities today, so I've done my part." Needless to say, praying for the homeless and giving money to charity are both worthy Christian acts. But sometimes I can use these acts as justifications for not devoting my whole self to Christian service. Perhaps Christ was not being figurative in the above passage. Maybe I should really ask myself, "When was the last time I consoled someone in prison or visited the hospital? How many truly destitute people do I know and how have I helped to ease their burdens?"

Here are a few related questions on which I could reflect:

- How much Christian service am I currently doing now? For example, do I write letters to prisoners? Do I visit the lonely elderly in nursing homes? Do I work for a homeless shelter? Do I bring food to shut-ins?

- In my job or school, do I keep an eye out for those who never seem to fit in? Do I invite them out to lunch occasionally? Do I stop by their desks to say hello from time to time? Or do I trash those same people by participating in daily gossip?

- Have I been Christ for my family lately? If so, how? How often have I sacrificed my free time to spend time with a brother, or a spouse, or my kids?

- Do I treat my clients and business partners with honor and respect? Am I honest with them? Am I truly interested in their well-being?

- How have I treated the service personnel (the people behind the counter, driving the city buses, protecting the streets, cleaning the floors) today?

- Is the world (my office, my school, my home) a better place because I'm in it?

PRAYER IS TRANSFORMATION BY GOD

The previous chapter showed how this transformation should be that of further surrendering to God's lordship. As I grow in my prayer life, God will call me to become more and more selfless. Like John the Baptist, our personal mission statement should be "He must increase…I must decrease" (John 3:30).

- Looking back over the past month or year, how have I decreased while Christ increased in my life?

- How have I been transformed by God recently? How am I not the same person I once was?

- Looking back on my prayer lately, what corner of my throne is Christ currently asking me to give up? What, concretely, do I have to do in my everyday life to make that surrendering happen? Even more concretely, what first steps can I take tomorrow?

- When I visit those sick and imprisoned, for instance, who is it that I bring to them: my God or myself? Upon my exit, are those I visited saying to themselves, "How good is this person" or are they saying, "How good is God"?

- Who or what have I promoted by my words and actions this day? God? God's "little ones" (see Matthew 25)? Or myself?

- What was the primary deciding factor in the decisions I made today? What god called the shots in my life today? My own agenda? My own happiness? Or did I allow the Kingdom of Heaven to be my priority?

- St. Paul exhorts the Corinthians "that none of you will be puffed up in favor of one against another" (1 Corinthians 4:6b). Have I slandered and gossiped about others today so that my own image might be "puffed up"? Have I wrapped myself up in petty little turf-wars among fellow workers or classmates?

- Have I chosen to be an ambassador for Christ regardless of the impact it might have on my reputation? Have I willingly risked being unpopular or considered to be no fun because of my ambassadorship?

PRAYER IS RECOGNITION OF GOD

Samuel Johnson has written, "Most people need to be reminded, not instructed." As a Christian minister, most of the time I am not so much called to teach or to preach Christ to others, but to remind them of their own holiness. I am to call forth the Christ I see in others and to be a sort of mirror for others so that they may see the image of God that they are (see Genesis 1:27). True, mirrors are brutally honest; they reveal the lovely looks *and* the hairy warts, so I also must humbly expose evil where I see it. But most people are already painfully aware of their warts. What they usually need to be reminded of is the part of them that is holy and beautiful. As a matter of fact, our sins spring forth from our forgetting that we are the temples of the Lord (see 1 Corinthians 6:19). With the "new lenses" I have received from my prayer, I can recognize and reflect the Spirit of God that dwells in all of God's children.

- Where have I recognized God today? Whose face did God wear for me today? How did I acknowledge and reverence God in others once I did recognize him?

- Where did I not find God today? Whose face did I mis-read today? What is it that is clouding my true vision of this person? What do I need to do to clear up that vision tomorrow?

- How did I recognize and reveal God's presence in the ordinary things of this day? Which of my actions this day would have been different had I recognized God in all?

- Are those around me more aware of God's presence in them because of the way I treated them today? Or did my actions and words, and my non-actions and silences help to convince them that "God is nowhere" (see Chapter Fourteen)?

It cannot be stressed enough that all of these questions I am to ask myself at the end of the day must be answered not only honestly, but also as concretely as possible. I must really poke and prod actual moments of my day—conversations I had, decisions I made, words I did and did not say and actions I did and did not do. I must distinguish the moments of the day that were and were not of God.

Conclusion

Any prayer life that does not make me an instrument of God's saving action in the world is an inauthentic one. Even cloistered monks, who live lives of solitude, do not view their vocation as being set apart from the world. Trappist contemplative Thomas Merton writes:

> One of the worst illusions in the mystical life would be to try to find God by barricading yourself inside your own soul, shutting out all external reality by sheer concentration and will-power, cutting yourself off from the world and other men by stuffing yourself inside your own mind and closing the door like a turtle.... We do not go into the desert to escape people but to learn how to find them.[2]

And what do I do once I truly find people? I recognize, acknowledge, reverence, celebrate and reflect that spirit of God that I find within them. I do all this through every single word and action that I say and do in the course of an ordinary day. Only then will I live out Christ's calling for me to be the light of the world, shining forth the saving power of God and to be the salt of the earth, flavoring God's people with everlasting love.[3] Only then will "they see my good works and give glory to the Father in heaven."[4]

NOTES

1. *SpirEx*, 24ff.
2. Thomas Merton, *New Seeds of Contemplation*, p. 47.
3. See Matthew 5:13-16.
4. Matthew 5:13-17.

Seasoned Reflections and New Thoughts

As mentioned in the preface to this new edition of Armchair Mystic, the publisher and I made a decision to leave—just as it is—the content of the original text. Aside from a few minor changes, that is what we have done. However, since I wrote this book *twenty* years ago, I do have a few new thoughts on the topic. (Given the years of priestly ministry and the years of additional meditation in my own prayer life, it would be disturbing if I didn't have any new thoughts on prayer!). This chapter is my way of sharing with you, in a personal sort of way, my seasoned reflections on the content of Armchair Mystic. First, I will point out to you those insights of which I feel even more strongly than when I wrote the book. Second, I will present a few new insights that I would add, if I were to write such a book today.[1]

Original statements about which I feel
even more strongly

The first regards time commitments. On the one hand, I feel more strongly than ever that *it is not necessary to pray for great lengths of time*, day by day. Most experienced pray-ers find that 30 minutes of meditation/contemplation per day is sufficient. On the other hand, I'm more convinced than ever that *you must pray every single day*, without exception. You might be tempted to think, "It's impossible to pray every single day. After all, I'm a busy person and life is filled with unexpected interruptions." Indeed, in my own life, I have found that practically no other commitment can be maintained perfectly. But a couple of years ago, during a busy period of my life, I experimented with keeping a log in order to determine how many days I would be forced to skip a prayer period. After 500 days of consistent prayer, I stopped counting! So now, at the risk of offending, I say to everyone: if you're too busy to spend 30 minutes a day with God, you're probably busier than God wants you to be. To summarize, putting these two points together, I would say that beginners often make the mistake of praying longer periods inconsistently rather than adopt the wiser strategy of praying shorter periods consistently.

Second, I still strongly recommend that you *instill a bit of ritual* in your daily prayer time by praying at the same time every day, praying in the same prayer-chair every day, using the same gestures, objects and routines every day, and so on. For example, I almost always pray within minutes after waking up (after a cup of bold French coffee, of course. After all, I am a Louisiana Cajun!). I usually pray in the same recliner in my room. I usually begin my prayer by ringing a prayer bell and I end it with praying the Liturgy of the Hours. These routines are a comfort to me, and they transport me right back to the sacred space of prayer.

Third, while it is not necessary to do so every day, I still believe that *journaling should be an integral part of your prayer life.* For one thing, journaling helps to clarify what your soul might be saying to God and what God might be saying to you. This is important since meditation and contemplation can feel a little vague and hazy at times. It's hard sometimes to know what God and your soul are saying to each other. Although I usually save the journaling for after the prayer time, I sometimes find myself writing down just one or two lines right smack in the middle of the prayer time. I write, "Dear Lord, I sense that you might be saying to me...." Or "Dear Lord, I want to tell you....". Seeing these one-liners in black-and-white grounds the soul-to-God communication and gives me something to work with. Sometimes I later find myself sensing that the statement wasn't exactly correct or that I need to tweak it a bit. So I re-write it. This process lends clarity and solidifies my sentiments toward God at that moment. I also like journaling because it helps to look back into the past in order to get a context for the present experience of prayer. It helps me to see not only the trees of the last few days but also the forest of this phase of my spiritual life. And, from time to time, I spend time reading journal entries from way back, gazing at my life with God from 30,000 feet.

Finally, I still stand by my notion that contemplation, by definition, is about "leaning into being"—that in my prayer time, I gently lean away from cluttered content and lean towards intimate "being-ness" with God. As I said in the original text, my most intimate moments with my loved ones are precisely the moments that we are simply *being* with one another in quiet nothing-ness. The same is true for my relationship with God. More than any other time in human history, we have much to benefit from this shedding of sound and information input. When I wrote about this twenty years ago, smart phones hardly existed at all. The first iPhone was released six years after *Armchair Mystic* was published. Now, most people have a universe of data sitting in their pocket or purse. While this media revolution is wonderful in many ways, it has also had the ill effect of exhausting us and destroying our attention span, our ability to sit still, and our ability to listen quietly for wordless, imageless gestures from God, from creation or even from our own heart. Now, far more than ever, we need contemplation to rescue us from the gluttony of superficial stimulation and to lead us to the living springs of our salvation.

New Thoughts

If I were to write *Armchair Mystic* today, these are the points which I would add:

Using the Imagination in Prayer

Chapters 7 and 8 introduce the idea of using one's imagination in prayer. The suggestion is to try to visualize a scene from the Bible—perhaps imagining yourself as one of the characters in the story. For example, in the Gospel stories wherein Jesus is walking on water while the apostles are being tossed about in a storm at sea, you might want to imagine yourself as St. Peter being called out on the water or as one of the apostles who fearfully remained in the boat while Peter ventured out. This type of prayer is often called "Ignatian Prayer" because St. Ignatius wrote about the "application of the senses" wherein as you read a Gospel narrative, you try to see the characters, hear their voices, smell the smells, etc.

In teaching this type of prayer, I have found that people often feel frustrated when they "can't see anything" or "can't get into it." They feel humiliated and conclude, "I just don't have a good imagination."

I suppose it's true that some people have a more vivid imagination than others. Still, I feel that people who are frustrated perhaps are trying too hard or are being too self-critical. With a bit of practice, anyone can do this kind of prayer. Here are some helpful things to keep in mind:

• First, keep in mind that, for whatever reason, most people struggle to visualize the features of human faces. This is completely natural. If the faces in your imagination are fuzzy or out of focus, just keep going and don't let it bother you.

- Second, the point of this type of prayer is to get a sense of the *inner* experience of a character in this story. For example, regarding the woman who washed Jesus' feet with her tears and dried them with her hair, you are encouraged to feel the emotions that the woman must have felt in that moment. But again, people end up frustrated and saying that they don't feel anything. If you struggle with *feeling*, then try *thinking about feeling*. If you cannot feel the emotions that the woman might have felt, then relax and ask yourself, "What do I *think* she might have been feeling at that moment?" Then, simply name a few emotions that you think the woman might have felt and go from there. This "thinking about feeling" is a secondary (as opposed to primary) way of getting at the experience, but it works almost as well.

Note that in the above paragraph, I write, "relax and ask yourself...." Relaxing is important in prayer because getting upset and frustrated will surely highjack your attention. Even if you "aren't doing a good job at this," it's no big deal. The Lord has myriad ways of reaching you.

Frustrated people in my workshops are consoled when I describe my personal experience of this type of prayer, so let me do so here. Most of the time, I'm not able to imagine an entire scene from beginning to end as though I were watching a scene from a movie. In fact, my "scenes" wouldn't even be long enough to be considered "a movie clip." Honestly, it's usually better if I don't try for that length because my prayer would then cease being a prayer and would become a mental exercise. Instead, I try to imagine a sort of "photograph" of the crucial moment in the scene. Perhaps the characters in my "photograph" will move a little, but only a little. Media-savvy millennials send each other "gifs" all the time. These are tiny videos that usually last only two seconds or so. If you don't know what this is, google the words "funny gifs" and a thousand of these tiny videos will pop up— everything from cats sneezing to babies dancing. In my prayer, I don't experience movies or even movie scenes so much as something closer to these tiny "gifs."

The whole point of meditation is communication with God; we imagine these Bible narratives as a way of starting a good conversation with God. Therefore, after you've spent a bit of time imagining the scene, feeling the emotions of the characters, etc, you should then pull back from the imaginative exercise and have a conversation with God about what you've experienced. I call this the "so what?" of the prayertime. The forgiven woman felt tremendous liberation by the way that Jesus treated her. *So what* does that mean for you and your relationship with Jesus? You have had a good impression of how the woman and Jesus interacted, *so what* have you learned about how Jesus wants to interact with you? Speak to Jesus about that. My point is this: the imaginative exercise in the prayer is a means to an end, not an end in itself. The end is communication with God. Therefore, even if the imaginative exercise is going well, pull back from it after a while and have a conversation with God about it. That is the whole point of prayer.

How the seasons of your life affect the seasons of your prayer life

Consider the following story:

> Jorge and Lupita were married in 1959. By 1969, they had five healthy and rambunctious children. Needless to say, the 70's were a busy time for this young couple! There were so many things going on at the same time—baseball

practices, dance recitals, First Communion Masses, trips to the urgent care clinic for stitches and cough medicine. And there were many decisions to be made and situations to deal with: Child #2 seems to bully her friends at school. Child #5 is too sensitive. And Child #1 doesn't want to go to church anymore. And what high school will they attend? And finances are tight. And Lupita suspects she's not being paid as much as she deserves. And Jorge feels unfulfilled in his job and dreams of a career change. Of these issues, which should they engage in an aggressive way? To which should they apply a light touch? Which should they ignore for the moment? Pondering, debating and even arguing about these issues was how Jorge and Lupita spent most of their alone-time together. Sometimes they spent hours lying in the dark in bed working through some tricky family problem. Thankfully, they loved and respected each other well. Though their relationship was strained at times, they always managed to navigate these choppy waters together.

By the 90's, the children were grown and had moved out of the house. While each of them had their own life challenges, they were handling them well enough without a huge amount of help from their parents. And money wasn't so tight any more. So Jorge and Lupita found themselves with a quieter and more peaceful life. This newfound settledness changed the way they spent time with each other. They could finally get a full night's sleep. They didn't have to spend so much time discussing and debating big decisions. After supper on any given night, they sat quietly on the back porch, listening to the radio and watching the dogs run around the yard. It was an easier, simpler time in their lives. While the 70's were exciting and adventuresome, they enjoyed this more tranquil phase of their family life.

But in 2000, their lives took another dramatic turn. Tomás, their eldest, moved back into their house, and he brought his two small children with him. Tomás's wife had moved away and was out of the picture. It turned out that she had a drug addiction and was out of control. And when she left, she took Tomás's money with her. Tomás was broke and paralyzed with depression. Lupita's and Jorge's quiet life vanished in an instant. As in the 70's, they found themselves steering the family ship through choppy waters. Again, there were issues to attend to and tricky decisions to be made. For now, anyway, there would be no more quiet evenings on the back porch.

But while this new phase of their life mirrored aspects of their hectic lives as young parents, this phase was different in some ways. First, they were grandparents of the young children of their house, which required a certain delicacy to their stepping into action so as not to usurp the role of the parents. Second, and more importantly, those tranquil years had had a profound and beautiful impact on the way they were present to their son and his children. Those years of quiet hours on the back porch had made them somehow wiser and more peaceful. They exuded a confident trust in God and in themselves as they approached the painful realities of their son's broken family.

Note how the seasons of their family life shaped the nature of the relationship of Lupita and Jorge. While their children were young, Lupita and Jorge were "partners" in the demanding "business" of raising a family. They spent most of their time together strategizing and working through the challenges of family life. Later, when their children were grown and independent, Lupita and Jorge were mature lovers and friends, enjoying each other's company in a relaxed and relatively trouble-free manner. But then things shifted again and they had to pivot their relationship— rolling up their sleeves and getting to work again, but now with a seasoned wisdom and grace.

Now imagine that Lupita had begun a contemplative prayer life before she was married and that she was faithful to her prayer life through the decades of her family life. How would the varied seasons of family life affect her prayer life? If the shifting demands of family life changed the way she related to Jorge, would it not also change the way she related to God in prayer? Indeed it would! During the tricky and difficult times, her prayer time would be spent discerning, pleading, and maybe even grieving. During the tranquil periods of their family life, she probably enjoyed a more contemplative—that is, peaceful, quiet, content-less moments with God.

The beginning of *Armchair Mystic* speaks of how people have the misconception that only monks and nuns are called to meditation and contemplation. The very title of the book implies that anyone quietly sitting in one's favorite armchair can be a contemplative. As the book explains, to pray contemplatively simply means to gently move towards quieter, simpler, less cluttered prayer. But this doesn't mean that as you mature in your prayer life, you'll do less and less "spiritual work" in your prayer time such as discerning about tricky situations of day-to-day life. So while it is true that a contemplative pray-er "leans into being" in her prayer life, she might also go through life-challenges wherein she will need to bring the nitty-gritty of her complicated life into her prayer.

How can both be true? How can I move closer and closer to "being" in my prayer while at the same time, spiritually working out tricky life-issues? This question gradually worked itself out in my own prayer life in the years following the publication of *Armchair Mystic.*

I wrote *Armchair Mystic* as a theology grad student in preparation for priestly ordination. My studies leant themselves naturally to contemplation since they demanded hours of reflection and bookwork in the solitude of my room. To study theology on a higher level, one must live an almost monastic life. But after ordination (and the release of *Armchair Mystic*), my young priestly life was anything but monastic. I was the director of pastoral ministry at Strake Jesuit, our large Catholic high school in Houston. And a few years later, I found myself the director of novices for the Jesuits, helping young men discern the most important decision of their lives: whether or not to profess vows as a Jesuit. On becoming novice director, my predecessor in the job said to me, "You are now a professional discerner—it is your profession to make and to aide in life-altering discernments."

From the monastic life of a theology grad student, to the hectic life of a high school priest, to the "heavy" life of novice director— how did these dramatic shifts in my daily life affect my prayer life? Tremendously so! As a grad student, I could enjoy the luxury of coming to Christ with empty hands, with nothing on my mind and heart but my grateful intimacy with God. As a high school priest, my prayer was more "hectic," reflecting the hectic nature of my work. "What, Lord, should I preach about at the upcoming Kairos Senior retreat? I need a homily right-quick, Lord!" And later, as a novice director, my prayer life contained slow, steady, thorough Ignatian discernments of vocations. It had neither the "monasticism" of my grad school prayer life nor the "frenzied-ness" of my high school ministry years.

Only now, as I'm writing this, am I realizing that the books I wrote in each of these periods reflected the compatible natures of my day-to-day life and my corresponding prayer life: While in my "monastic" grad school years, I wrote about "lean into being" in *Armchair Mystic.* During my frenetic high school years, I wrote about "taking the nitty-gritty of my daily life into my prayer" in the book, "*God, I Have Issues.*" And during my years of heavy discernment as a novice director, I wrote about Ignatian Discernment of Spirits in *God's Voice Within.* Each season of my daily life shaped the season of my prayer life and unconsciously shaped the content of my writing!

Now consider: if after a relatively quiet period of your life, you find yourself having to re-enter a more active stage, as happened for Jorge and Lupita as grandparents, do you then have to abandon your "lean into being" contemplative prayer life? Not at all. After you've had some good solid years of contemplative prayer, you reach a state of inner stillness in your prayer that does not go away when your life demands that your prayer become a bit more active. Note that when Jorge and Lupita had to return to a more active life, they did not do so as the frenetic young couple that they were in the '70s. All those years of quiet nights on the back porch had had a permanent effect on them. While on the exterior they became more active, they did so out of an interior core that was peaceful, still, confident, hopeful, and trusting in God. The same would be true of your prayer life if you had to return to more activity after years of more content-less contemplation.

To use a different metaphor, entering into a contemplative prayer life is like entering into a spiritual desert: vast, still, seemingly empty. Journeying through this desert your soul learns to draw water not from rivers and lakes but from a mysterious inner oasis that even you can't see or perceive. And yet you know it's there because you are thriving in this desert.

Returning to a more active prayer life wherein you must bring concrete situations and discernments into your prayer is *not* turning around and exiting the desert by the way you came. No, it is coming to an active city *on the other side* of the desert. There is a spiritual land on the other side of the desert wherein you are now back among people and places and activities, but you are there as an entirely different person—as a *contemplative in action*, to use a favorite self-description of the Jesuits and of followers of Saint Ignatius. You are now a monk in the city.

I have chosen to write about this in this new edition of *Armchair Mystic* because I do not want the reader to get the impression that a contemplative pray-er becomes an other-worldly mystic. Just as you began your contemplative journey not in a monastery but in your baby-bottle-stained armchair, so your contemplative prayer life turns and returns to command-central of a busy and demanding life from time to time. But now everything is different. You are back in action, but now you are a contemplative in action.

TIME TO SAY GOODBYE

Ok, that's it! To the *Armchair Mystic* girls and guys out there: thank you. Thank you for allowing me, through this book, into the sacred spaces—the nooks and crannies of your quiet and intimate daily prayer. As an invited guest in your sacred space, I am keenly aware that I am on holy ground and that God is present in a special way. Thank you for welcoming me here. It has been a blessing to my life and I promise to pray for you as you continue to reach God by reaching *for* God.

Mark E. Thibodeaux, SJ
March 23, 2019

LIVING A PRAYERFUL LIFE
God in the Details

There are two ways to live prayerfully in your everyday life. The first is to pray around, in and through the ordinary activities of your day. The second is to cultivate a contemplative lifestyle.

THE FIRST WAY: 'PRAY ALWAYS'[1]

With a little creativity, you can find many ways to interweave your life with prayer. Here are ten suggestions:

1. It is easy to pray ready-made prayers throughout the day because they require less concentration and take up less time. Beginning the day with the Morning Offering, and taking little breaks during the day to pray the Liturgy of the Hours, the Rosary or the Angelus has enhanced Chris-tians' daily lives for hundreds of years.[2] Today, many people are returning to the practice of going to daily Mass. Church parishes sometimes offer convenient Mass times for people on their way to and from work or on their lunch breaks.

2. Meal times provide an opportunity to praise God for his many gifts. A Jesuit community in Cambridge, Massa-chusetts, pauses between their entreé and dessert for a communal prayer wherein individuals verbally thank God for some concrete blessing of that day. This type of prayer could easily be adapted to various family get-togethers.

3. Before communicating with anyone, one can pray for that person. I developed a little habit of making the Sign of the Cross with my thumb over the addressee of my outgoing mail as a way of blessing the recipient. One could develop similar habits with phone conversations, appointments and so on.

4. From my grandparents' generation, I learned to "offer up" any pains, difficulties or sacrifices of the day. If your back is aching or you have a headache that won't go away, you can ask God to make your quiet acceptance of the pain a prayer for some intention of the day. You can do the same with unpleasant or tedious tasks such as grading papers or mowing the lawn.

5. One of my strongest memories of my grandmother is her insistence that we begin any trip by saying the rosary. We were always well into the first decade before even leaving the town limits!

6. From my dad, I learned that anything can be blessed. After his long days of soybean or wheat planting, he would return to each field to say a short blessing over it. A wise teacher taught me to pray over my grade-book by prayerfully touching each name therein. When I was a kid, my mom prayed over my aching junk food-laden tummy. While driving on the freeway, I sometimes pray silently for the strangers I see as I go by. When I am traveling and staying in a guest room or an AirBnB, I usually say a prayer over the room before I leave, asking God to bless the next person who stays there.

7. A favorite slogan of my mom is "A family that prays together stays together." That is why she routinely gathered my dad, my four brothers and me together for a Bible reading or the rosary.

8. Making the Sign of the Cross is a wonderful little ritual. Many Cajuns do so upon hearing the siren of an emergency

vehicle as a way of praying for whoever is in trouble. My Cajun elders also "sign themselves" every time they drive past a church as a reminder that God dwells among his people.

9. I like to keep a small dry-erase board nailed to the back of my closet door so that I'm the only one who would notice it. On it, I write a word, phrase, Bible verse or quote that will remind me daily of whatever grace I am presently bringing into my boat. Holy cards and prayers on stickers or magnets can also be helpful in this regard.

10. It's good to be engaging in spiritual reading continuously. Catholic publishers now have great spiritual books in small sizes that you could fit into your purse, briefcase or book bag.

THE SECOND WAY: A CONTEMPLATIVE LIFESTYLE

Besides finding various moments in your day to pray, you should do what you can to live a contemplative lifestyle. As much as possible, every moment of your life should be quiet, peaceful and relaxed. Just as there are a myriad of ways to bring prayer into your day, so there are many little behaviors you can adopt which, while not being explicitly spiritual, will aid the soul to remain in a more reflective state.

1. *Live Naturally.* Find ways to convene with God's creation. Frequent a city park. Sit under a tree. Go to the country. Walk through a field. Stick your feet in a stream. Also, show your gratitude for creation by making efforts to clean up the environment.

2. *Live Simply.* Resist the temptation to acquire lots of stuff. There is a story of a distraught businessman who went to spend a few days of retreat in a monastery. The kind monk who showed him to his cell said to him, "I hope your stay is a blessed one. If you need anything, let us know and we'll teach you how to live without it."

3. *Live Healthily.* Saint Paul calls the body "a temple of the Holy Spirit" (1 Corinthians 6:12-20). Make sure you maintain your temple with the reverence it deserves. If your body is not in shape, your prayer will be hindered.

4. *Live Orderly.* Clean your room. Make your bed. Pick up after yourself. Genesis tells us that part of God's role is to bring order to chaos (see Genesis 1). You should do the same with the little waters of chaos in your own life. You will find that your mother was right all along: cleanliness is next to Godliness.

5. *Live Richly.* Read, write, paint, dance, sing. Learn to play the xylophone even if it is more noise than music; so long as it is joyful noise, the Lord will dance to it (see Psalms 95 and 98). Stimulate the artistic side of yourself. It is the part of you most willing to surrender control to a higher power.

6. *Live Ascetically.* Look at all of the activities of your day that bring you instant gratification, everything from junk food, to unhealthy Netflix shows, to your third beer, to promiscuous behaviors. Now ask God to help you transcend them. They do you no good.

7. *Live Slowly.* Every now and then park your car in the slot farthest from the door. Give your zippy email a rest once in a while and write someone a real letter. Take the stairs instead of the elevator sometimes. Calm down. Jesuit moral theologian Father James Keenan is fond of saying, "If I drive to work aggressively and speedily, I eventually arrive at my office with the same manic personality that brought me here." Learn to amble—to wander off. The world won't fall apart because you didn't accomplish all of your little goals of the day.

8. *Live Reflectively.* Whenever you walk or drive past a church or chapel, stop and check in with the real Boss. Take advantage of

days of reflection offered by your church. If possible, take several days off and make a silent retreat.

9. *Live Lovingly.* Begin with yourself. Jesuit Father John Powell says, "People who truly enjoy being who they are always have good company. They are with someone they like twenty-four hours a day."[3] Forgive yourself. You're not the monster you think you are. And for God's sake (and your own), learn to laugh at yourself often. An ancient Chinese proverb says, "Blessed are they who laugh at themselves. They shall never cease to be entertained."

10. *Live Sacrificially.* Find some wonderful cause or causes to give yourself to. As Saint Francis of Assisi said, it is in giving that we receive.

Notes

1. Luke 18:1.
2. If you are unfamiliar with these prayers, any Catholic bookstore or even a simple Google search can provide you with them.
3. John Powell, SJ, and Michael H. Cheney, *Path Through Christian Living* (Allen, Tex.: Tabor Publishing, 1994), p. 95.

appendix b

··

RESOURCE RECOMMENDATIONS
My Favorite...

...Books on beginning to pray contemplatively

Green, Thomas H. *Opening to God*. Notre Dame, Ind.: Ave Maria Press, 1977.

Hermes, Kathryn. *Beginning Contemplative Prayer*. Pauline Books, 2011.

Hauser, Richard J. *In His Spirit: A Guide to Today's Spirituality*. Mahwah, N.J.: Paulist Press, 1982.

Keating, Thomas. *Intimacy With God*. New York: Crossroad/ Herder & Herder, 1996.

Laird, Martin. *Into the Silent Land*. Oxford University Press, 2006.

...Websites

FranciscanMedia.org

IgnatianSpirituality.com

Jesuits.org

Usccb.org

W2.vatican.va

...Apps

Pray as you go

iBreviary

Insight Timer

Mass Times

Saint of the Day
Bible Gateway
Reimagining the Ignatian Examen
Examine

...Books by Mark E. Thibodeaux, SJ

God, I Have Issues: Fifty Ways to Pray No Matter How You Feel. Franciscan Media, 2011.

God's Voice Within: The Ignatian Way to Discover God's Will, Loyola Press, 2010.

Reimagining the Ignatian Examen: Fresh Ways to Pray from Your Day. Loyola Press, 2015.

...Resources for finding retreat houses and spiritual directors

The internet
Your local Catholic bookstore
Your local diocesan office
Your local convent or monastery
A prayerful priest, nun or lay minister in your home parish

SCRIPTURE SUGGESTIONS
My Ten Favorite...

...Old Testament Passages with which to Pray

Deuteronomy 1:29-31

"The Lord your God carried you, just as one carries a child."

1 Samuel 3:1-10

"Here I am."

1 Kings 19:1-13

God speaks in the "sound of sheer silence."

Psalm 51

"Create in me a clean heart, O God."

Psalm 131:1-2

"my soul is like the weaned/child that is with me."

Psalm 139:1-18

God's providence.

Isaiah 11:1-9

"The wolf shall live with the lamb."

Isaiah 49:8-16

"I will not forget you."

Isaiah 58:1-12

True fasting and sacrifice is living justly.

Ezekiel 37:1-14

To the dry bones the Lord says, "I will cause breath to enter you, and you shall live."

...Gospel Passages with which to Pray

Matthew 6:19-34

True riches/ against worry.

Matthew 11:28-30

"Come to me, all you that are weary..."

Mark 4:35-41

Jesus calms the storm.

Mark 10:46-52

"My teacher, let me see again."

Luke 7:36-50

The forgiven woman anoints Jesus.

Luke 9:10-17

The multiplication of the loaves.

Luke 15:11-32

The Prodigal Son.

Luke 24:13-35

Jesus appears on the road to Emmaus.

John 1:35-39

"Rabbi...where are you staying?"... "Come and see."

John 15:9-17

"I have called you friends.... [L]ove one another."

Printed in the United States
By Bookmasters